To my horse loving
friends the
Wagemans

Hooves of Thunder

Thunder Agard,
A First Racehorse Experience

Enjoy the ride

By

Rebecca Anderson

Becky Anderson

Book design by Rebecca L Anderson

Rebecca Lynne Anderson Books are available for order through Ingram Press Catalogues

Disclaimer

This memoir of Rebecca Lynne Anderson is true to the best of her knowledge and memory. Most names were not used and some characters are composites of several people with the same job. The racing statistics are available online at Equibase.com. Rebecca cares deeply for all the race track people and means no disrespect to anyone.

Rebecca Lynne Anderson
Visit my website at www.buggybecky.com

Printed in the United States of America
First Printing: February 2018
Published by Sojourn Publishing, LLC

ISBN: 978-1-62747-226-5
Ebook ISBN: 978-1-62747-227-2

Dedication

This book is dedicated to all the good people who make the wonderful sport of horseracing possible—From the dedicated breeders and owners of horses, to the veterinarians, trainers, riders, grooms, and stable hands caring for the horses daily. The jockeys are one half of this athletic endeavor, and are most necessary as they bravely guide powerful animals at top speed. Three cheers to the race track management, security, grounds keepers, dining and wait staff, and bet ticket takers who make the entire experience so enjoyable. I learned that racing is a big, complicated process that involves the cooperation of thousands of people and horses. This book is for them all.

Acknowledgements

A special thank you goes to Thunder Agard's trainers, Fred Danley and Cesar Cornejo, who held my hand and walked me through everything. They held my horse's welfare above all else, and had my complete trust. They listened to my worries and complaints, then went on to do what was best.

I want to thank Tom Bird for giving me the confidence to complete this book that I needed to write. Thanks to Jessi Irick of Blue-Line Editing for her help.

Extra love goes to my husband who indulged all my ups and downs of authorship with caution and support. He always knew I could, and he gave me whatever I needed; a push or a hug.

Finally, I want to acknowledge the special horse that made it all possible, Thunder Agard. He is a "once in a lifetime" horse who now lives at our farm as my extra special riding horse.

Chapter 1

"Are you going to leave that kid here?" Snapped the wiry old man. He sat resting in a wooden chair on the porch of the old white farmhouse. His granddaughter was already in the front yard. She was pulling on the lead rope of a silver dappled pony with a new sorrel colt by her side. The marc kcpt hei head down and grazed as Becky brushed and played with her, trying to get the foal to come closer so she could pet him, too.

"She wants to. She asks me a hundred times a day. It sure would make my weekend easier with the baby and toddler," replied his daughter in a tired voice. She was overwhelmed with her husband working swing shift and it was hard to keep the kids quiet. Leaving her oldest daughter with her father was something she had recently fallen back on for relief.

Grandpa Agard kept Becky many times, so he saw no problem letting her stay this time as well. He took her everywhere he went.

Grandpa Agard was never addressed by his first name. It just wasn't proper for children to do that in the era he grew up in. He had been born in the farm house in 1913, was poor and farmed the homestead piece in eastern Kansas. He raised large ponies that were smaller than horses but big enough for an adult to ride.

"I raise these ponies because I can ride them to work, work all day long and ride them home on no feed." Grandpa Agard explained to Becky as she played in the front yard. By "no feed" he meant he didn't have to buy grain or extra hay to keep them fat. Just grazing was enough. He was a small man, 5'4" and 115 pounds all his life. He had made extra money jockeying in match races at the fairgrounds in his younger days. To Becky, who was only seven, he was a big and wise horseman whom she idolized.

He had married and raised a family during the Great Depression, so thrift was an important part of his life and ponies fit the bill. He had known lots of hard times and disappointment, but his big dream was to have his own racehorse. One week, early in April when Becky was staying with Grandpa Agard, they loaded up his prized Thoroughbred mare to take her to be bred. He called her Beauty but Becky thought she was a rather ugly big black horse. She was tall with a long face, long skinny neck and big feet. Her real name was "Cup O' Luck." What a weird name, Becky thought.

"Get in the Jeep and let's go! It's a long trip to Salina," Grandpa Agard hollered. Becky climbed up into the truck hitched to the horse trailer with excitement. Grandpa told Becky all about bloodlines and why he had chosen to breed to this stallion as they drove across the flat prairie. It nicked with his mare's bloodline and that was important, he said. She didn't know anything about what he was saying, but loved his enthusiasm. Grandpa Agard had saved money for two years to afford this breeding and had high expectations for the foal to be a winning race horse that he would train and race at the county fairs. Becky was alone on this trip with Grandpa Agard because she wanted to go while all the others in his family thought he was crazy. They'd heard this story a hundred times. Pipe dreams, they said. But Becky hung on every word and they sank deep into her soul. He was her hero.

They arrived at the stallion farm about noon. It had fancy pipe corrals painted white, and a huge red and white barn. The barn was bigger and fancier than Grandpa Agard's house. They were greeted in the driveway by the owner. The stallion was brought out by a groom. The stallion was big and brown, immaculately groomed, and impressive looking. Becky didn't remember his name, but the owner rattled off his bloodlines and winnings with great pride as the groom moved him up and down the driveway. The adults walked into the barn office and Becky stayed outside. A deal was made. Becky saw a handshake and Grandpa paid the man.

The soft elegant voice of the stallion owner purred, "She'll be fine, just come pick her up in a couple months." Beauty was unloaded and lead away by a groom into a paddock near the barn.

Becky spent most of the summer with Grandpa Agard on his farm with the ponies. The Agard's had a herd of fifty pony mares of all colors, and a bright sorrel stallion with a white mane, tail, and a big white blaze down his face. The stallion's name was Major.

They raised ponies for Grandpa Agard's stagecoach ride at Joyland Amusement Park. He had eight matched teams, all sorrel with white manes and tails. He sold most of the foals every fall but kept a few of the right color for his teams.

Grandpa told Becky which ponies in the pasture near the house were broke to ride, but offered no help for her to ride one. He said, "If you can catch one and bring it up here to the porch, I'll help you get the saddle on." Then he just sat down in his chair on the porch in the shade. Becky headed to the pasture with two hay strings and a pocket full of pellets. She walked for hours following the ponies. Eventually, she wore them down and she could catch one to ride. She learned patience. Grandpa just sat and watched. He hardly ever told her how to ride or what to do. "You learn by doing," was his reply.

By late fall, Becky had graduated to riding Tony the Pony, a beautiful black and white paint. Tony knew tricks she didn't know. As Becky was riding along the path in the pasture, when he thought it had been long enough, he would lie down and fall over on his side. The first time, Becky jumped off. "Oh no, Tony, are you hurt?" He immediately jumped up and ran to the house without her. When Tony got back to the house, Grandpa Agard knew Becky was walking home. Funny thing, Grandpa Agard never came looking for her. She was miffed. She could be hurt or snake bit or something. Shouldn't she get sympathy?

After a week, Grandpa Agard brought out a little riding crop with a handle to go around her wrist. "Next time Tony lies down, swing the crop two times hard on his butt and hang on tight." Grandpa Agard carefully instructed Becky. She was scared, but determined not to let that ornery pony get the better of her; or let Grandpa Agard think she couldn't ride. She was tired of walking home. When he lay down at almost the exact spot as the days before, she swung the whip. Swish. Pop. Up Tony jumped. She almost fell off, but clung to the saddle horn asTony trotted down the lane. Becky never had to use the whip on him again, and she learned a valuable lesson about the need for a riding crop.

Beauty had the run of the farm. The best pasture, called the east 80, was knee deep in grass and had two natural spring ponds with trees around them. Beauty shared it with the pony herd. As her belly was getting big and round, Grandpa Agard was making plans and picking names. He explained to Becky how race horse's names often indicated their sire's line or a famous ancestor or a mix of the sire and dam's names. He wanted a horse colt. He said he thought that they usually raced better. It was the happiest Becky had ever seen Grandpa Agard.

Beauty was due to foal in April. No baby came, but she looked pregnant. We just had to wait until the foal wanted to come. Grandpa Agard said it was not unusual for first time mares to go two weeks overdue. Two weeks passed.

"It's not unusual for horse colts to carry longer. Everything looks fine so we will just wait on her," Grandpa told Becky. But Becky noticed him getting snappy at people, and then he went quiet. Beauty had been moved up to the 5-acre lot beside the barn where she was easier to watch. The end of May came with no foal. Grandpa Agard became angry. He stomped when he did the chores like he never had before.

The first week of June, Grandpa Agard became even more angry. He went around the farm yelling and cursing and kicking things. Everyone avoided him. The next week, he was quiet, refusing to talk to anyone. On the third Saturday in June, he called Becky up to the front porch. She was riding one of the ponies around the front yard. "Becky, I'm going to give you Beauty's first foal for your very own."

"Wow," Becky squealed. She was so excited. She had been checking the mare several times a day for two months. "Really Grandpa? He will be mine?"

"You bet. I think it's exactly what you need," he said with a little too much enthusiasm.

Becky was over the moon. Her own horse! And not just a pony! It was a giant step up for her. She anxiously waited for Beauty to foal and checked her even more often. The grass was lush. It was so hot outside, but Becky sat out by the barn for days wanting to see the foal born. One morning in July, she went to the barn and there he was, already standing up and nursing. He was absolutely beautiful to Becky. He was chocolate brown with a white mane and tail, and a big blaze down his face.

Becky ran to the house to tell Grandpa Agard to come see the new colt.

"I never want to see that damned colt," he growled fiercely. Becky turned and ran back to the barn, too excited to notice her grandfather's pain. She never questioned why Grandpa Agard had given her the colt. Beauty was loaded in the trailer when her colt was three months old, and Becky never saw her again. Her name was never ever mentioned again.

Grandpa Agard's dream for a race horse had been crushed, but the seed had been planted deep in Becky's heart. That's why she named *her* race horse Thunder Agard.

Chapter 2

The dream of a race horse had been planted subconsciously in Becky, but it had to lay dormant for many years. Thoroughbreds were not the horses that met Becky's needs as a young married woman with five children and a full time veterinary practice. She wanted her children to love horses as much as she did, and want to ride. Ponies and horses of all varieties came and went as the children's skills developed and the family budget changed. They eventually graduated to Paints, Quarter Horses, and a Mustang. The family enjoyed the tar out of them at 4-H shows, roping, family trail rides, and buggy driving.

Years passed. Becky bought one Thoroughbred stallion off the track when a race meet closed. He was a beautiful, graceful, bright bay with four white feet and a blaze. That must have been influenced by memories of her first horse that Grandpa Agard had given her. However, he was lazy and never ignited any dreams for Becky, so he became someone else's Hunter show horse.

Through her work as a veterinarian, Becky saw hundreds of horses a year. They were nice, but they were just horses to her. She had an excellent memory for horses. Becky loved all horses and all the different things they could do if they had a place and people who loved them. Occasionally, a horse would quicken her heart and make her want to own that horse to fulfill its purpose. One of her clients had just such a horse. Every year she visited their Thoroughbred farm to vaccinate and de-worm about fifteen horses. Only one caught her eye and pulled at her heart strings.

The mare was a bright red bay with a big white star in the center of her forehead. Becky could tell by the way the mare moved around in her small corral that she was athletic. She bucked, reared, and flipped her tail over her back to prance around before they caught her. The mare had raced well in California with moderate success. She had been purchased for the New Mexico bred program.

If a horse is bred and the foal born in the state, with both parents enrolled in the program, they have special races for the New Mexico Bred; plus, higher purses and bonuses for the breeder and owner. It's a great plan for the state as well as for racing.

"What are you going to do with that mare?" Becky queried politely.

"We are going to breed her. She is registered in the New Mexico Bred program and so is our stallion. She's got good bloodlines and our stallion goes back to Mr. Prospector," the farm owner stated proudly.

"Great! I'll be excited to see that baby," Becky answered enthusiastically with a big smile on her face. She truly wanted to see her clients succeed with a good race horse.

The next year no foal came. Over the next five years, no foal was born. Becky wanted to see what that mare would produce, and the mare was reaching midlife, which is late for a first breeding. She inquired about her every year:

In 2008, the winter was hard; Hay was expensive and hard to get. One day, the farm owner came to Becky and stated, "I know you always liked that mare. Would you be interested in buying her?" A little spark made Becky's heart flutter. The timing was good. The children were all grown and on their own. Yes, she wanted that mare.

"I'm not sure, I'll have to talk to my husband. How much do you want for her?" A price was quoted, maybe a little high if the mare was barren, but within Becky's budget.

Becky begged her husband. "I was offered that Thoroughbred mare I always liked today." No need to say which mare she was talking about because Becky mentioned every year that she liked her and that she still hadn't foaled yet.

"What are you going to do with an old Thoroughbred mare?" quizzed Frank.

"I want to raise a racehorse of our own. You know this New Mexico Bred program is really growing," replied Becky excitedly.

"You know what a money pit that is, don't you? Have you ever known even one person that's made money in racehorses? Why didn't they ever breed her if she's so good?"

"But, honey, I want her. It's not about the money. I don't know why but there is something special about her to me. She looks like the old-fashioned Thoroughbreds of the 50's and 60's. I don't have many horses left. I could sell something else to make room for her." Becky pleaded.

"Ok," Frank melted. "If that's what you really want go tell them tomorrow we'll take her." He would do anything to make his wife happy (within reason), and nothing lit up her face like a horse did. If Frank asked if she wanted a new pair of diamond earrings or this horse, he knew she'd choose the horse. That's why Becky didn't have fancy diamond earrings.

The next weekend, Becky, her daughter, and her son-in-law hooked up the old white gooseneck stock trailer and went to pick up the mare.

"Be careful," the old horseman cautioned. "She's really hard to handle. Don't come in the pen 'til I catch her. She rears, especially when you feed her."

"Ok." Becky knew she had been on the track for a few years, so she had to have been handled a lot in the past, but it had been several years since she had been off the track.

The owner haltered the mare and led her out of the pen. The mare had a kind eye and gentle expression. Becky took the lead, and the mare followed obediently to the stock trailer. She jumped in like she had done it hundreds of times. When Becky got her home, she turned the mare out in a large arena so Frank could see her. She pranced and bucked and ran loops around the pen. Her conformation was so balanced. Yes, she could rear! She could stand on her hind legs and walk half way across the pen. That is a very difficult and athletic maneuver. It takes years to teach a Lipizzaner to do that and it's his crowning achievement. Yes, Becky was pleased as punch to have her. Mostly she was gentle around people; she never kicked or struck or tried to hurt anyone. At feeding time, she did insist on her food coming first, so stay out of her way. Becky always threw her food in from outside the pen.

Now the anticipation of getting her ready to breed started. Her name was "Time out Tiger" but Becky called her "The Mare," so all the family called her that as well. She was de- wormed and vaccinated. She had a Coggins test for Equine Infectious Anemia, which is required to transport horses in the U.S. She had her Caslicks removed; a surgery done when she was racing to close the skin over the vulva so air isn't pulled inside when running. This showed that the previous owners had never tried to breed her, or it would have been removed already. She looked shiny and healthy, ready to breed. Now it was a waiting game until spring.

Becky spent hours studying the mare's pedigree and her famous ancestors. She was a descendant of Northern Dancer, who raced in the late 60's when Becky was in high school, and who she had seen race on TV. She studied which lines crossed well and which of those lines were available in New Mexico. A lot had changed in 40 years, but Thoroughbreds still require a live breeding. The pages of the New Mexico Horse Breeders Magazine had folded pages and turned down corners. Which one did Becky like? Which one could she afford? Where were they located? There were so many questions to answer.

"Honey, look at this one." Becky held out the magazine to her husband.

"I really don't care. You know I don't know anything about the bloodlines. It's all your decision." Frank answered as he looked at the picture of a Thoroughbred stallion.

"I know, but I just want you to see all the choices we have," Becky cajoled him as she took back the book and flipped the pages. "Your opinion matters to me."

Becky decided she wanted to breed The Mare to a Storm Cat son. He was the leading sire of all race horses in the US and all his sons had half of his genes. There were a few Storm Cat sons standing in New Mexico. She looked at their pictures, poured over their pedigrees, and asked about their temperament as well as the temperament and record of their offspring. She had heard that some Storm Cat descendants had bad tempers and were aggressive, and she wanted to choose a milder mannered stallion. Weatherly Farms in southern New Mexico had a good reputation, worked with a good veterinarian, and had two Storm Cat stallions Becky liked. Their stud fees were very reasonable, and with mare care and vet fees she calculated that she could afford to breed. She called for an appointment and delivered the Mare, Time Out Tiger to the breeding farm.

When Becky got to the office, they called to the barn where two grooms got the stallions out and paraded them for her to see. It brought back such memories of going with Grandpa Agard to a farm where a groom brought out a stallion. She looked at both and asked the grooms which was easier to work with. Choices to make… Becky pondered and wished someone else would help her make the decision. Then on a gut feeling that she wanted the gentler stallion she made up her mind. Distinctive Cat would be the sire of her new racehorse foal. He was solidly built and well behaved. The mare was easy to breed and pregnant and ready to go home in sixty days. Becky waited another month so that the long trip home wouldn't interfere with the pregnancy.

When Becky arrived to pick up her mare, she was in a very large paddock with about twenty other pregnant Thoroughbred mares, mostly bays and browns. The office manager gave the groom a number and off he went to bring The Mare out and load her up. All the mares had a belt-like collar around their necks with large number tags on them. The collars are put on at arrival and not removed the entire time the mare is at the breeding farm so that no mix ups occur. In general, one bay Thoroughbred looks like another, except to people who know them well.

As Becky waited, she looked around. In the round pen outside the stallion barn stood another horse that made her heart flutter and excitement fill her. He was a big, dappled grey stallion that was one of the most beautiful horses she had ever seen. Becky had seen tens of thousands of horses in her life and only a few that she coveted. His head was chiseled and looked like the old Sam Savitt drawings. His eye was large, dark and kind. His neck arched beautifully over the top rail of the pen. His dappled coat sparkled and made him look like a show horse. He was so tall Becky was standing on a hay bale outside the round pen to scratch his ears as he leaned against her. At 17.2 hands, he was much taller than most race horses. He was a very social friendly horse, and liked people to pet him. She got his advertising flyer saying he was To Teras the son of UNBRIDLED SONG, one of the leading sires in the US. The grandsire UNBRIDLED had won the Kentucky Derby. To Teras was unraced due to an injury the flyer stated. He had no statistics, but lots of unrealized potential. Most breeders do not recommend breeding to an unproven horse. Becky didn't care. She wanted beautiful. She wanted silver dappled. She wanted a horse exactly like this one. Why hadn't she seen him first? She drove home with her mare carrying a Distinctive Cat foal but wanting a To Teras foal. All the way home, alone in the truck, Becky plotted how to get to breed the mare again to this grey stallion with the super friendly personality.

"Honey, I saw the most amazing horse today. He took my breath away and made my heart skip a beat. We need to breed to him next year. He's at the same farm and they treated us so well."

Frank moaned. "What is wrong with you? Never satisfied? You've only been home an hour and already talking about another foal. I thought you said you wanted a race horse not many race horses." He was trying to be so stern but the sparkle in Becky's eyes and the flush on her cheeks told him he had already lost.

Chapter 3

Summer, fall, and winter passed smoothly, and as spring approached, their schedules got fuller and fuller with obligations that took them away from home. Frank, always the planner for the worst-case scenario, worried. "What are we going to do about this mare in foal? We have too much invested to not be here when she delivers. She's a maiden mare and all kinds of problems could come up. Who's going to do that?"

"Let's take her back to the breeding farm to foal her out. They have around the clock observation and lots of experience. We could also breed her back at the same time. Remember, that's where TO TERAS is standing. Please, it's a worry off our plates if she is there being watched." Becky reasoned to her husband.

So, in the middle of March, thirty days before the foal was due Becky drove the mare back to Weatherly farms to foal. The people there remembered her and were happy to see her return. They already had several foals on the ground and the watch teams were in full swing.

The office manager asked as she was filling out the papers, "Do you want to breed her back on the foal heat?'

"I thought about it, but I really wanted to breed to TO TERAS and I don't think I can afford it right now," Becky answered regretfully.

The office manager smiled broadly. "What luck for you. His owner wants more colts on the ground and is breeding proven mares for half the regular stud fee this year."

It seemed like a sign to Becky that they should breed the mare again, so without even asking Frank, she said yes. "Ok I can do that. Do I need to pay anything up front?" she offered, remembering from her childhood Grandpa Agard's deal.

"No, we bill monthly for mare care and vet care with the stud fee due when a live foal is born." The manager explained.

"What a deal. Let me sign the breeding contract. I really want a horse exactly like him." Becky was happy as could be and almost floated home. One foal due within a month and one for next year, too. The drive home with the empty trailer took five hours, but Becky hardly noticed. They were too busy with other projects to even miss the mare.

She foaled easily and the farm sent pictures of a nice bay filly. She had one white hind foot and an off-center star on her forehead. It reminded Becky of a poem Grandpa Agard had taught her.

"One white foot, buy him.
Two white feet, try him.
Three white feet, pass him by.
Four white feet, let him die."

It didn't mean much to her but it had always stuck in her mind. When horses were a family's only transportation and necessary for their livelihood, hoof color may have been the difference between hardship and survival. This filly was big, strong boned, long legged, and looked like a race horse.

The mare was bred again and became pregnant with a foal for next year. Since horses are pregnant for eleven months and a week, they usually become pregnant right after one foal is born for a spring foal the next year. It's nature's way, and not a hardship on a well-fed mare.

The farm called when an ultrasound was done at eighteen days pregnant. Frank and Becky decided to leave her for ninety days to be sure she would stay pregnant on the trip home, and the new filly could grow a little to travel better. Becky was excited to know she had one on the ground and exactly what she wanted on the way.

One late afternoon in June, she got a call from Weatherly Farms. Unusual, she thought. They don't usually call unless there is a problem.

"We are having a problem with your mare. She is colicky," the farm veterinarian said. "I've given her Banamine and tubed her with mineral oil and water about an hour ago, but she's still painful and wanting to go down."

"What do you think we should do?" Becky asked.

"We want to send her to the Equine Clinic near the track where they have specialists and all night staff," he replied.

"Ok, go ahead. Be sure to give them all my contact information and have them call me after their evaluation. Give me their number, too, so I can call them. Thanks for all that you are doing. I really appreciate it."

The dreaded C word. For horses, colic is one of the most painful and unpredictable disorders to affect them. It can have many causes and only a few solutions. Untreated, it is frequently fatal.

The Equine Specialty Clinic called at about 7:30 in the evening, and Becky spoke with a very knowledgeable young woman veterinarian. She said the mare had not responded well to pain medications and was not passing stools. She was in serious condition. The veterinarian wanted to connect the mare to intravenous fluids and possibly consider abdominal surgery for a displaced colon.

Becky agreed "Yes, go ahead and give her fluids but we are not going to do surgery." Becky knew that colic surgery was very expensive, often more than the value of the horse, and only had a fifty/ fifty chance of recovery. That was too big a gamble for Becky to be willing to take. "How is the foal doing?"

"She's in the stall with her mom and doing fine. She is very calm and nibbling hay in the corner." The vet replied.

The vet called again at about 10:00 PM after 30 liters of fluid had been given to say her status remained unchanged. Becky asked, "How much is her bill now? What do you think are her chances of survival?"

"Well, that's hard to tell. Her bill is around $1,500, and she hasn't changed in the last four hours. If fluids don't help, I'd say it's serious and I recommend surgery," the veterinarian counseled.

"No, I don't want surgery. I'll be down to pick her up as soon as I can. How early is someone there in the morning? Can I pick her up at 6:00?" Becky responded.

"I don't get there until seven, but we have a veterinarian in the barn all night."

"Ok, I'll be there." Becky hung up the phone

Becky told her dear friend, who is also a horse lover, that she was leaving to go pick up her mare in Anthony, New Mexico right then. Her friend was working at the veterinary clinic and offered to go with her. Becky was glad for the company. Her friend is Swiss, exacting, competent, and capable, with a common sense "get it done" attitude. That made her a great asset as a traveling companion. She knew exactly how Becky felt. It's what she would have done if it was her horse.

They hitched the old white gooseneck stock trailer to the big truck, filled up with diesel, and headed down the road at 11:00 PM. It was a five-hour drive, mostly on four-lane highways, except in town near the clinic. Becky rolled many thoughts over in her mind. Why am I driving all night to pick up my mare if she is at a good vet clinic? For one thing, I am the best darn veterinarian I know, and I care more about this horse than anyone else. I know what she needs and what I'm willing to do. I already have all the supplies needed. If the mare is going to die, I want her at home. Plus, I'd have to make a trip to pick up the filly anyway, so I might as well make the trip now. Becky was good at rationalizing what she wanted to do. Just two old ladies heading down the interstate at midnight; normal, right?!

Her friend thought it was a little crazy, but she didn't want Becky to go alone. Becky was wound up and talked for almost two hours. Her friend was tired after working all day, and she mumbled answers as she dozed on and off.

Where was Frank during this situation? He was staying home to work the vet clinic. They still had the only veterinary clinic for a 60-mile radius to help all the local people whose animals would need care. He had given Becky the unbelievable gift of freedom by staying behind to work all day. Frank would be so worried while the women were gone, but he put on a brave face for the public. Some people didn't understand, but Becky did and loved him for it. He had given her his love and trust to allow her to do what she felt was best. Most men would have just said no, but Frank knew that would crush his wife, and he had deep respect for her and her decisions.

The drive was long. It was dark and Becky's butt hurts. Her foot was tired on the gas pedal. She didn't use cruise control when pulling the trailer because it gave her less control and slowed reaction time. With a big trailer, things can get into trouble fast. Luckily, this trailer was old and solid. It's a gooseneck which means it hitches in the bed of the truck over the rear axle making it easier to pull. Becky had pulled this trailer thousands of miles to all kinds of events, from 4-H to carriage driving shows to hauling mares and foals. They zipped down the highway.

Becky and Monica visited a while, then Monica snoozed a little. She was a very early riser, so she slept and got up before Becky in the morning. Becky was a hoot owl anyway and frequently up until 1:00 in the morning. She started getting tired about 3:30, but wasn't sleepy because of the worry. The scenery between home and Las Cruces was not much to look at, and it was dark anyway.

With good luck, no flats, and enough gas, the two women arrived at 4:30 at the vet clinic. Becky parked the truck and trailer then walked into the barn to look at the mare. The barn was well-lit.

The mare was alive, head down, on an IV drip, but not rolling or in enough pain to thrash. Her heart rate was elevated to 75bpm, but her mucous membranes were pink. The foal was sleeping in a big pile of straw in the corner of the stall. Becky went back to the truck to sleep after she had seen the mare. Monica went to the practice track beside where the truck was parked to watch the early morning workouts.

The track was well-groomed. The sun was just starting to rise and mist rolled over the ground. It was breathtaking. She stood near the outside rail, watching the exercise riders go by. They must have thought she was a rich owner or very important person because each one said, "Good morning ma'am" as they rode by. Some of the colts were hard to ride, cantering sideways and fighting every step. Some were being ponied with a rider up and some floated by beautifully like in a dream.

When Becky woke up, she walked over to watch, but soon noticed one of the vets heading in to do morning rounds. She followed him to the barn. He did a pulse and respiration and listened to the mare's abdomen. He did a rectal exam, where they put their arm inside the rectum of the horse as far as they can reach, to feel the intestines that may be dilated or displaced, bands, or tight places in the internal organs. He did this all in the stall without tying the mare up. Becky thought in her mind how dangerous this was.

He must have sensed her stare and thoughts because he turned and said, "She is so gentle and well-behaved, and I've done these three times tonight without tying her. Feels like a displaced colon. No change all night, but it's not my case, so Dr. Stevens will be here in thirty minutes.

Dr. Stevens arrived right on time in her white coat, blood work in hand, and looking very spiffy and fresh. She explained what she thought, what had been done, and why the mare needed to go to surgery. Becky nodded and listened. She thanked the veterinarian and told her she had done a good job, but she was taking the mare home now.

"Did you drive all night to get here?" Dr. Stevens questioned.

"Right," Becky replied.

"Are you driving home now?" she asked.

"Right," Becky repeated. "Just as soon as you give her another dose of Banamine and I pay the bill. The fluids are almost finished. Please leave the catheter in place in case I need it on the way home."

Becky didn't mean to be short, but didn't feel much like socializing. They had done their job and she had made her decisions. Becky brought her own medical bag with what may be needed on the trip home. She settled in the office, loaded the foal, then the mare, and tied her long in case she wanted to lie down. They had bedded the front compartment before they left with two bales of shavings and one bale of straw on top. There was plenty of room and no place for her feet to get caught if she were to lay down. The foal was loose so she could move to get out of the mare's way.

Becky drove carefully out of town, slow and gentle around the corners. Once on the highway, it was smooth sailing. The mare stayed on her feet the whole trip. With the sun shining in her eyes, Becky wasn't falling asleep and had a good visit with her friend on the way home discussing all the problems they had each had with horses in the past, and which decisions had been good or bad.

Becky prayed the mare would live and not lose this pregnancy. She believed in Divine Intervention if asked for. This was the horse she dreamed of. This coming foal was sired by the horse that had touched her heart. Distinct Off Center, the foal by her side was nice. Becky had high expectations for her, but she wasn't "the one"; the dream horse. It would be a miracle if the mare didn't slip this pregnancy. Becky had no more control over the outcome, so she had to trust that the right thing would happen. As Becky pulled into the driveway, Frank came out and took over the unloading of the horses, as well as stabling and unhitching the trailer. Becky thanked Monica for going with her on the trip, and they both went straight to their rooms to sleep. It had been a stressful twelve hours.

Within hours of getting home, the mare was eating grass hay and moving around freely. She started pooping like a goose all over everything.

The pregnancy survived. They were back in the race horse business. Becky called a week later to tell the manager and veterinarian at Weatherly Farms that the mare and filly and pregnancy had all made it home safely and alive.

"Thank you so much. I worry, but often I never hear a thing. Good luck to you." Everyone always said "good luck" in the racing industry for everything.

Chapter 4

Off Center, the Mare's first foal, was weaned and her training was started. Fall and winter passed uneventfully. In April, Becky was watching the mare closely. One morning, when she went to the paddock to feed, a new stud colt had been born. He was plain bay, no white at all, scrawny with one front foot turned slightly out. As soon as Becky saw him, disappointment started to well up. Tears filled her eyes. Not gray. Not pretty like his father. This wasn't what she had planned and waited for all year. Then, she distinctly heard Grandpa Agard's voice: "This IS a race horse. Good things are often small, and perfection doesn't always win." She wrapped her arms around the foal's neck, buried her face in its fuzzy mane and cried tears of overwhelming emotion. Not joy, but something. Maybe disappointment. Maybe a connection to Grandpa Agard's dream.

Becky had already decided to name the colt Thunder, and Agard was added because he was the race horse Becky's grandpa never got to have. She had felt Grandpa Agard's spirit during the drive to get the colicky mare, and again when she saw the scrawny little guy as a newborn. Thunder Agard was tough and small, just like his name sake, from the first week of his life.

As the little spindly bay colt ran circles around his mother in the foaling paddock, he had no idea that he had been given a big name before he was born, or that it came with big expectations. He pranced and kicked to get his dam's attention as she stood calmly chewing her breakfast of alfalfa and sweet feed. He reared and pawed his tiny hooves on his dam's Shoulder, but she just moved over and ignored him. He did have the attention of Becky, his breeder, who gazed disappointedly at the plain brown colt. No white star or marking on his legs. His bone structure was delicate and one front foot toed out slightly. That didn't stop him from showing off his athletic ability.

It's just that Becky's expectations had been so different from the foal she was watching. She had specifically chosen the mare because of her classic Thoroughbred look and large correct bone structure. Her large white star accentuated her classic head and red bay color. The colt's sire had been selected on the spur of the moment because his classic beauty took Becky's breath away. He was the most perfect horse she had seen in 50 years of being associated with horses. He was very tall, with a chiseled head, and a sparkling dappled grey coat with a black mane and tail. He was extremely friendly and sought attention from anyone who was around.

Why was this foal born small, fine boned, and plain? His fluffy black tail flipped as he ran. His brown body was bouncing and turning in the corral. He didn't know he was plain. He just looked ordinary. No white markings, no unique identifying looks. He was plain. He looked like hundreds of other Thoroughbreds. He was not at all what Becky had dreamed of.

As he grew, his attitude and personality set him apart. He would approach Becky, touch her arm with his nose, then wheel around and run off, flipping his tail as he went. He would return slowly and try to push her out of his space with his butt. She just stood and waited. He stared with deep brown eyes filled with curiosity and a little mischief. Becky could scratch his shoulder if he felt like it but he could race off any time he wanted.

As Thunder grew, he went through the gangly yearling stage of all head and legs, though he still raced around his paddock, turning and rearing with extreme athleticism. He had been trained to lead, get in and out of the trailer, be groomed, and have his hooves trimmed. The farrier tried to turn the right foot in as he trimmed, but it still turned out a little like the minute hand at five after the hour.

As a two year, old, Thunder started to look like a TB racehorse. He had matured some and had grown into his legs and head. He was a nice, rich bay with black mane, tail, and legs up to the knees; a pretty color, but still the most common among Thoroughbreds, so he didn't stand out. His head was straight with a wide forehead, intelligent eyes, and large nostrils to intake lots of air. Plain standard TB.

He was friendly, yet pushy. He liked people, like his sire, but wanted his own way. He played most of the time, but he loved the training for racing because he got to be with so many other horses. He teased the horses in the stalls on either side of him, and shook his head when they snorted at him.

The trainer was impressed by how well he took to the track, and his strong work ethic to try whatever they asked of him. He ran hard when asked and slowed when asked.

Becky and Frank went to see him at the racetrack and hardly recognized him the first time he worked in the early morning. He had smooth lean muscles and a gleaming coat. After a few minutes, they recognized him by his distinct movement, prancing, and strong and alert and readiness for fun. It wasn't his physical appearance that made him noticeable, but his personality and actions.

After the workout, back at the barn, he had been washed and was on the walker with five other horses; three browns, a gray, and a chestnut. At first, it took a careful look to pick him out, but then he bucked and reared a little, then pranced, all full of himself. That was Thunder showing off. He had become a favorite at the barn because of his personality. Some of his sire's friendliness was starting to show.

The phone rang about 8:00 on Saturday morning. Frank answered and was quiet, looking solemn. "That was our trainer. Thunder was hurt this morning during his workout. Fred is sending the veterinarian to examine him, but he said it didn't look good." Frank told Becky, who was watching him expectantly.

"Oh, no. He hasn't even raced yet. How could he be hurt? What kind of hurt?" Becky asked getting louder with each question. Her chest tightened until it was painful. Her belly hurt. The worst may have happened. She knew it happened to other people, so why not them? It wasn't the first horse they had ever lost. There was Cecilia's Orange and Becky's favorite, Silver Bullet. She turned her head so her husband couldn't see the tears rolling down her red cheeks. She didn't want her husband to know how weak she was to cry over a horse; or for him to think that it hurt her so much that they should just stop having animals. He knew her well after 36 years, and loved her so much that he just wanted to protect her from the pain.

"Let them get x-rays. Whatever it is, let's just wait and see," Becky mumbled. "Those track veterinarians know what they are doing and have lots of experience with injuries."

"No, I'm going to pick him up right now," Frank stated bluntly. "No sense letting them put him down at the track. I'll go get him and bring him home to the farm." He walked rapidly to the truck to go hitch the big white stock trailer so that his wife didn't see how upset he was. Frank needed to be in control of the situation.

"Do you want me to go with you?" Becky asked, hoping he didn't want her to go. She didn't want to make a scene in public if she could help it. But seeing Thunder hurt at the track where he had been so happy just a few days ago would probably push her into a tearful mess.

"No, I can do it myself. I'll call you from the track when I get there and let you know what I find out after I talk to Fred and the veterinarian." Frank pulled out of the driveway, alone with his own thoughts–most of which were how to soften this blow for his wife who had such big dreams for a racehorse.

"In here," Fred the trainer called to Frank when he saw the trailer pull up near the barn Thunder Agard was in. The trainer's concern was for the horse, but he also didn't know the Andersons very well yet, so he was not making any recommendations one way or the other. He had been a trainer for many years and had experience with horses breaking down. He knew some didn't recover, and it could sour owners if it was their first horse. He had only been their trainer for a few months, and over the years he had learned to avoid saying much until he knew what the horse owners expected. They ranged from absentee owners to family pet owners. Fred was soft spoken and steady.

"He's sedated with Torbutrol and Banamine. Two vets had looked at the x-rays. It's a fractured sesmoid, outside right front. Both thought he probably won't be a race horse, but surgery is an option." He waited to hear the response.

Torbutrol is a potent narcotic pain medication with sedation effects, and Banamine is a non-steroidal anti-inflammatory medication like aspirin, but much stronger. The leg was wrapped in a solid three layer Robert Jones dressing that's almost like a cast. The other front leg was wrapped for support. Frank looked him over, noticing the sweat on his neck and the pinched nostrils and tense eyes. He felt the bandages, which were on solidly. He had applied the same bandages many times in his career as a mixed animal veterinarian in a small town. Thunder was standing on 3 legs with his head down and the toe of his right front foot barely resting on the ground.

Frank and the veterinarian discussed the options. One: euthanasia because he would be in pain. Two: surgery to screw the sesmoid bone together and keep it confined to see if he'd be sound later. Three: Keep it wrapped or cast and let nature heal it enough that he could just stand around. None were very good options, but he'd discuss them with Becky at length. She was very in tune with what was best for her horse. She would not allow any horse to suffer unnecessarily, especially not one she had raised.

"I'm here. He is standing. What do you want me to do?" Frank phoned Becky from the shed row where Thunder was stabled. The others had moved away to give him room to talk to his wife.

Becky had pulled herself together a little bit better. "Just bring him home, and we'll bury him here. I can't think right now. Give me a little more time."

"OK, I'll load him and leave Albuquerque now," declared Frank.

Becky had some time before the horse would be home. Her heart was sad. Her belly ached like she was about to vomit, but she was strong. She let logic and work take over. She felt like they could give him a chance, so she had to get a small stall ready with lots of bedding so Thunder could lie down. She used two bales of sawdust with one bale of straw on top. There was an automatic waterer in the corner. Her thoughts raced ahead. It will be too late in the day to put him to sleep when they got home that afternoon. A hole had to be dug with the backhoe.

"Shit, I don't even know if the backhoe is working right now. Damn, I'm so angry that I can't seem to get a race horse," Becky shouted to nobody. She understood her grandfather better at that moment. The yelling made her feel better.

As the trailer pulled into the drive, Frank called out the truck window, "Where do you want him?"

"Right here, it has the automatic waterer, it's close to the hay and it's small. He'll be safe until morning and we can decide what comes next." Becky watched Thunder stumble out of the trailer and limp into his small pen. That was not fun. Not the excitement racing was supposed to be. Thunder looked sedated but brighter than Becky had expected. His eyes were relaxed and he was standing comfortably on three legs. Luckily, he wasn't a big horse, and in racing condition his weight wasn't against him.

"OK," Frank groaned "We'll just wait to see what the morning brings." He was tired and stressed from the drive back. That night they lay curled in each other arms supporting each other. Frank drifted off to sleep, but Becky just lay quiet, pretending to be asleep. Her muscles were all tense and a sad story played over and over in her head. She prayed and sang to herself but didn't sleep for a long time.

A beautiful sunrise greeted Frank the next morning. Frank, who was always the first one up, went out to feed. Becky hadn't fallen asleep until about 3:00 AM and was slow to get out of bed. When Frank came back in, she was sitting in her chair but not dressed. "Well, how does he look today?"

"Went to his feed, but he's not moving much. He's lame, but doesn't look too bad. He's protecting that leg really well," Frank reported.

Becky sighed. "Good. I'll go look at him. No sense changing the wrap. It's a strong one and they are expensive to replace. Was the wound open?"

"It was already wrapped when I got there, but they said there were no marks on the skin at all."

That was a sign in the horse's favor. He wouldn't have an open wound infection to worry about on top of the fracture.

Becky dressed and started outside then turned around. "Let me get the Banamine so he won't hurt while we decide what to do." She reached for the medication, needle, and syringe.

At the stall, Frank stepped up and took the injection from Becky. "Let me give that, Honey. He may be spooky about IV's." She held Thunder's head, but he stood like a show horse and never flinched a bit.

Later that afternoon, he was looking around the pen and nickering to all the other horses, but stayed standing in one spot. A little hope crept into Becky's voice. "He's looking for food. That's always a good sign. And his friendly streak is coming back. How can we put him down now? Let's give it a little more time. Time is cheap. I won't let him suffer, but maybe he'll be able to heal enough to just walk around."

Frank snorted. "Well what the hell do you want with a pasture ornament? I don't think high-strung thoroughbreds make the best pets."

"All the polo horses I worked with were Thoroughbreds and they were not high strung. They could be very cooperative and easy to ride. Plus, I'm not ready yet," Becky stated. "He doesn't look that stressed. Give him the Banamine. I'll hold him." She rubbed his forehead. "Good boy Thunder," she murmured as he got his next injection.

Thunder was off the grain he received at the track to help get the "high" out of him. He was eating hay like a baby pig, cleaning up every scrap. He was still getting his Banamine pain medicine IV twice a day. He had started moving around his small pen quite a bit. He could do whatever he felt up to in the small pen. Thunder looked for the other horses and called to get them attention. He had enjoyed having stall mates on either side that he could talk to at the track. The wrap was still strong, tight, and firm.

At two weeks, the wrap needed to be changed. Becky changed it in the stall. Off with the old. Not much swelling, not much heat over the fetlock. Those were both good signs for Thunder. A new support wrap was applied with lots of cotton, two six-inch brown gauze, and a vet wrap. The wrap was solidly firm. The good left leg got a new support wrap of cotton, one brown gauze, and a vet wrap because it was still supporting most of the weight. Now he occasionally put some weight on the right leg now.

Becky decided to decrease the Banamine to once a day. "We don't need ulcers on top of everything else. He sure is eating well. He nickers to me every time I walk by, asking for more hay." She felt better now about not having to put him down. He didn't appear to be suffering. "I think we can wait. I don't know what I'm waiting for exactly, but time is cheap."

"All he has is time. This sure shot his racing career, not a Kentucky derby contender now." Mirth filled Frank's eyes, "Hell," he laughed. "Maybe he'll be my riding horse. He *is* healing much better than expected." Becky laughed, too. Her husband hadn't been on a horse in over twenty years—although he had ridden in Saddle Club in his youth and was a darn good rider. He rode a motorcycle with his American Legion buddies now. Frank was a horseman, but he wasn't a cowboy.

One more month passed. Becky suggested, "Let's not wrap it again. He seems pretty stable."

"No, I think it needs a light support for at least two more weeks, maybe only on the right leg. Let's not start taking short cuts now." Frank chastised his wife. He often thought she took too many short cuts.

"He sure is bored in this little pen." Becky sympathized with Thunder as he moved around so she could change his wrap. He was not haltered or held. He touched his nose to her rear end as she rewrapped the leg.

"Too bad! He's not coming out of there for three months." Frank was always the stickler for going the extra mile and not cutting corners; a reflection of his military training early in his life.

Thunder had been injured in the fall, and as spring started to arrive, Thunder, now a three-year-old, started to get hormonally crazy. He was nipping and squealing and rearing in his larger pen. Although the fetlock was enlarged on the back outside, Thunder did not seem to favor the leg.

Frank stated emphatically, "We better geld him next week." Gelding is a surgery to turn a stallion into a neutered animal without male hormones. They are much safer and easier to handle. Most male horses are geldings. "He's off all the meds, so what we see is what we get."

"Let's do an x-ray to see how it looks when we geld him," Becky pleaded. "I didn't see the original and curiosity is bugging me."

"We already decided not to spend thousands on surgery," Frank stated flatly.

"But I want to know what it looks like," she whined.

"No, we are not taking x-rays. Let nature take its course. Whatever it is, it is. Period."

"But it's so hard for me not knowing," Becky pushed.

Frank shot back, "If you knew it hadn't healed properly could you put him down now?

"No," Becky answered quietly. "I just really, really want to know." Becky whined again like a spoiled child. She wanted some reassurance that the fracture was healed.

Frank was annoyed and getting a little angry. "Then get in that pen and feel it, rub it. You'll know all you need to know," he shot back as he marched back to the house.

Becky went into the pen and stood on Thunder's right side, scratching his withers. He cocked his head and wiggled his top lip in thanks for the rub on an itchy place. She ran her hand down the leg over the knee and around to the tendons. They were tight and firm down to the fetlock where the sesmoid fracture had been. She pressed on the bone and he only turned his head to snuffle Becky's hat. Except for the sesmoid bone being about 1/3 larger than the other sesmoid, no evidence of the injury could be seen. Thunder showed no signs of pain or lameness.

Chapter 5

The next week, Thunder was castrated inside his little pen with no complications and he began his mellowing out process. Now six months had passed since his injury. No wraps, no pain meds… playing and bucking in his pen. The right front fetlock was enlarged on the back side, but not hot or painful to the touch or moving.

"Open up the other side of the pen so he can move around more and see the other horses," Frank ordered, his old military training showing. He often didn't realize he was ordering and not requesting. Becky knew it was just his manner and was not offended. "He doesn't seem lame, but two excellent equine veterinarians thought he probably wouldn't race again. I want you to start looking for an alternative for him." Frank was tired of feeding a horse with no plan. He was much too structured to not have a plan. Becky could have just floated along waiting to see what happened without a plan.

"He's still holding his weight and shiny, so I don't think he's hurting. I can't see a limp. He turns right and left just fine," Becky observed enthusiastically.

The partition gate was opened, which tripled the space he could move around in as well as added four new corners to look out. One month later, he was still sound after being in the larger pen where he was much more active. Becky's mind searched for an alternative use for Thunder.

"Hey, Honey, he's not too big. He'd make a great barrel racing horse for some girl who knows how to ride. He's gentle on the ground. How about Natalie? She has run barrels for years and her horse is getting up in years."

"Okay, Becky. Let me talk to her husband first. I don't want to get anything stirred up if he doesn't want her to have another horse. Are you OK with giving him to her?"

Natalie was a spoiled woman with the fanciest equipment and the fanciest truck and trailer. She went to barrel races almost every weekend and was quite a good rider. Becky was a little jealous of all her stuff and free time to go to rodeos as she pleased. It would chafe her to give her horse to Natalie, but she knew it would be a good home. Plus, Natalie could afford a trainer for Thunder.

"I don't think any of our kids can take a horse right now, and the grandchildren need a much gentler horse than Thunder. Yes, I think it's a good fit for him. She takes good care of her horses," Becky reasoned.

A few days later Friday, Becky made the call. "Natalie, I have a nice little Thoroughbred, 15'2, that can't race but is sound. Do you want to look at him for a barrel prospect?"

"How well is he trained?" Natalie queried politely.

"He's right off the track, but he had four months training and they said he was gentle, never bucked. He is very friendly and has nice ground manners. I don't even halter him for grooming. He loads easily in the trailer and stands for the farrier. Come look and see what you think. I want him to have a good home where someone can use him."

Natalie never came. She never looked. She wasn't interested in a project, even if it was free. Becky wished she would have at least looked then told Becky no, he's not what she wanted. Becky's feelings were hurt. Her horse wasn't even good enough for a look. Ignoring is not less hurtful than the truth. Oh, well, so she wasn't interested. Becky toughened up and moved on. Maybe someone else would want Thunder.

Becky asked all her children if they had any idea that they might want to do something with Thunder. Clay had been quite a team roper before marriage; children and the job took up all his time and money. "Yeah! I still have several friends with arenas who rope all the time. He's quick and heelers don't have to take much weight." He spoke enthusiastically. In team roping, a very popular cowboy sport in the Southwest, one man on a horse ropes the steer's horns and pulls the steer around. That horse must be strong and stoutly built. He's called the header. The heeler catches both hind feet, pulls the steer out straight, then let's go. Heelers should be in the right place at the right time, so speed is more important than weight. Becky thought Thunder could do that, and the young athletic cowboys wouldn't have any trouble training him. "Sure, talk to all your roping buddies. If they'll come get him, I'll give him to them free."

Becky and Frank never heard a word from any of them. Nobody came to pick him up. Nobody wanted to invest the time and work it would take to see if he had potential. Sometimes a good horse cannot even be given away. Sadly, that happened to many Thoroughbreds. Becky could not believe how hard it was to give away a horse.

What was to be done with a non-racing small Thoroughbred? The young girls who used to ride hunters, take lessons, and show every weekend, had almost all gone away. The poor economy, uninvolved parents, and the time a horse takes ended most of that activity. No hunter barn was willing to take him. Becky called several that she'd known from her days riding hunters a long time ago. They had schooling horses out their ears to feed. Nobody wanted a lesson horse because they didn't have enough lessons to keep them in the money.

Becky pondered and worried. Then she became frustrated. They had saved Thunder, but for what? Could he just stand around and eat and take up space? They couldn't afford a "pasture ornament." She decided he could become her riding and driving horse—if she had help training him. Although she had trained many of her own horses, she knew older people didn't bounce when they hit the ground. Thunder was so very quick, his spins and jumping sideways could unseat her even if he never bucked. Becky did ground work (and more ground work) with the saddle, but was afraid to get on him because of her round bottom and lack of athleticism.

They decided to send him to their favorite Amish trainer in Colorado. They called and he told them, “I’ll take him, but not right now. It’s still cold up here and I’m busy foaling. I’ll take him in two months. It’s $1200 a month with a three-month minimum.” He had trained two other horses for them and they were very pleased with the outcome. It was expensive, but it was a plan. Thunder had a future. At last, a plan.

Chapter 6

Summer had arrived. Becky had more time to play with the horses she loved. Thunder looked great, fat and shiny with no signs of lameness. "Let's turn him out in the big paddock for a while."

Frank watched as Becky led him up to the big paddock. Five acres fenced with netting on all sides. Amazed, Frank sighed, "Look at him run. He wants to run. He loves to run. Let's leave him here for a while before we take him to the trainer."

After two weeks of running out in the paddock, it was clear that Thunder was not lame. There was no heat in the pastern, though a small hard lump over the right sesmoid could still be felt. Frank was excited. "Wow! Sound. That's a miracle. Nobody seems to want him. Why train him for a riding horse? He wants to run. Let's put him back into race training and see what happens."

Becky had lost her enthusiasm for racing and was afraid of what could happen, but agreed to give it a try if they started slowly and could back out at any time. She had anxiety over building up hope and getting hurt again. The original racing trainer in southern Utah was called to see if he could condition him, as well as evaluate his speed and how the leg would hold up. They both trusted Brady's judgment and honesty to put the horse first. Brady worked out of the county fair race track of the small town where he lived. He had been a very successful young trainer in California when his life changed paths. With a wife and children, he realized that the nomadic race track life wasn't what he wanted his family. He graduated as a radiographic technician and moved to a small town to work in their hospital. It was an excellent environment to raise a family. However, the race horse bug never leaves a person. Before long, he started training a few horses for different owners and sending them to tracks in Arizona and California. His reputation grew with each success. He was the first person to saddle and work Thunder Agard. He taught him the starting gate and got him into running condition as a two-year-old. He thought Thunder had the makings of a real class race horse.

Frank made the call. "Do you remember that colt you started for us last year?"

"Sure, the one with the broke sesmoid," was the first thing Brady said. He had heard all about the injury through the racetrack grapevine, but didn't know what had become of him.

"That's the one. Would you consider taking him back for conditioning and training? It's been almost a year and he's sound now. We want to know if he can race again." Frank explained.

"I'll give him a try but there are no guarantees," explained Brady. "I'll tell you right off the bat if he can't hold up to the work." That was exactly why they had chosen to return him to Brady. He would take his time and be honest with them about the horse's ability and soundness.

Three months later, Becky, Frank, and some friends traveled to Utah to watch Thunder race in the 4th of July County Fair meet. The trip was fun. The small town had a big 4th of July parade down Main Street with floats, bands, dance groups, horse-drawn wagons, tractors, and clowns.

At 1:00, the races started at the fairgrounds. Thunder was in the third race with six horses. Brady and his son walked him to the saddling paddock and boosted the jockey up. He stood well in the starting gate. He made a clean break and ran like he loved it. He placed third. After the race, Brady met with the Andersons over BBQ lunch and stated, "This is the same horse I started last year. He wants to run and has some speed. I worked him hard and didn't see any pain or lameness. I'd take him back to New Mexico while I've got him in good shape and get him on the track."

That led to another conversation with Fred, the trainer in New Mexico. "Fred, do you remember the colt Thunder Agard that you trained for us last year?"

"Yup, broke sesmoid," was all he said. There was a pause as Fred waited to see what Frank wanted.

"Well, we've had him in Utah conditioning and want to try him again on the track. Would you train him for us again?"

Fred was cautious. "Well, we'll see how he trains. Maybe you'll get six or eight races before he breaks down for good. No guarantees."

Becky and Frank had a lot of faith in Fred. He was an older trainer with many years of experience who wasn't influenced by others to do anything that wasn't best for the horse–funny that the young trainer and the old trainer talked and thought alike. Both were multi-generational racehorse people with their own lingo. Both trainers had honest reputations; no gimmicks, no drugs, and always put the horse first.

"We will rely on you to tell us when and where to run. We trust your experience and knowledge." Frank and Becky started making plans to pick him up and haul him to Fred's barn in Albuquerque. From Grants to Utah to Albuquerque was a big trip. It was one year that month since Thunder had been injured. Becky felt comfortable that they were doing the right thing.

After five weeks of training, Fred called to say Thunder was doing well and they were going to "do a work'" the next morning. That means they run the horse hard and fast for 4 furlongs, or half a mile. The time and rank of the horses working that day is posted on the computer. Thunder was 10 out of 34 horses that worked that day at that distance. He was at the Downs of Albuquerque. The surface of the track was good, but that was the same track where he had fractured his sesmoid one year earlier. Cesar, the assistant trainer, told them he had done well and had worn support wraps on his front legs. Cesar was the main connection between the Andersons and the racetrack. He was a tall, lanky Hispanic with a quick big smile, who liked to talk to the owners about their horses. His career had started as a morning rider with aspirations to be a jockey until he grew too tall to make the weight of jockeys. He was the one that usually rode Thunder in the mornings. Becky liked his calm manner with the horses and his willingness to take the time to explain things to her. He easily straddled the two worlds, speaking fluently in Spanish to the grooms and jockeys then easily switching to English to talk to Becky and Frank.

Becky was nervous, worried, She couldn't concentrate on any work, wondering how Thunder was after his first work. Frank couldn't help but notice her tension, so he suggested the next morning they drive to Albuquerque to visit the barn and feel the leg for themselves.

The track security guard checked the owner badges to let them on the grounds. That was done so random people aren't roaming around the barn area. Thunder nickered when he saw Becky approach his stall. Maybe he recognized her—or maybe he just wanted more food. Cesar saw them walking to the barn and met them at the stall. "He worked good and cooled out nice," he told them. Frank and Becky both felt the leg. Cool, firm, no lameness. All was well. It was such a relief that, after a nice lunch, they drove home happy and comforted.

With fall racing in full swing, Fred said he'd start looking for a race for Thunder Agard. He was specifically looking for a New Mexico Bred, three–year-old maiden race with a low purse so the competition would not be too tough. The race would be just young horses instead of more experienced older horses. Maiden means horses who have never won a race, and NM bred means both parents are in New Mexico and the colt was born there as opposed to Kentucky or California. It's a great program to keep the value of local horses, and Becky was proud to be a part of it.

The trainer picked the jockey who would ride in the race. Trainers have a close relationship with jockeys and know who they think will do the best job for each horse. Some jockeys only ride Thoroughbreds and some only ride Quarter Horses because they have completely different running styles. Frank and Becky came to watch a few morning workouts and became acquainted with the rider who would be Thunder's jockey. This rider always dressed flashy: pressed pants, expensive belt, tight polo shirt, and a helmet with his name on it. He was around thirty, Hispanic, and a very good rider. Becky thought he showed a lot of confidence. Some people thought he was arrogant, but Becky liked his style; confident, flamboyant, and ready to win. He was always polite and friendly to them. He complemented their horse as he rode past them back to the barn. The next time they came, he wasn't at the track. He was not riding Thunder.

Becky asked the groom, "What happened to our jockey?"

"He's not here," was the reply.

"Why? Where is he?" Becky queried again.

The same reply "He's not here." Owners are outsiders and not privy to information. The track people are like a family in some ways, closemouthed to outsiders and gossips in the circle. Becky never knew what became of that rider.

Soon, Fred found a race for Thunder that was exactly the conditions he wanted. Another jockey was selected. He was a young Anglo jockey who was the son of a jockey. He was taller than some and a little cocky, but friendly and had a good race record.

As race day progressed, and it got closer to their race, Becky's anticipation built. She started to worry. Will he lead up to the saddling paddock ok? Will he stand quietly to be saddled and not waste all his energy before the race? So many things could happen. Just as one race ended, the horses walked up to the saddling paddock for the next race. It was a grassy circle with numbers on the ground corresponding to each horse's number. There were twelve open front box stalls numbered for the horse's position. Thunder was #7, near the end. He was one of the last horses to show up. He was led around the circle by his groom once, then into his numbered box. Fred was standing in the box stall. Cesar and the groom were leading and holding Thunder. Becky walked out to stand on the # 7 where the owners stand to watch the saddling. Cesar put on Thunder's numbered saddle blanket, which was orange.

Each number has its own color which is the same color in every race at every track so the bettors can tell where each number is on the track. The color also matches the jockey's helmet cover. Next, they put the tiny little saddle that belongs to the jockey on the horse.

Each jockey uses his own saddle that is fit, broke in, and adjusted just for him. Next came the tight stretchy overgirth that takes two people to put on. It won't slip because of a soft rubber piece under the girth. Fred and Cesar worked together to get it on just right. Thunder stood quietly and was easily saddled. Becky was smiling from ear to ear with pride because of her horse's good behavior. One chestnut horse in the race had to be moving all the time and they were trying to saddle him while he walked. That was not easy, nor was it safe.

Thunder's front legs were wrapped with red and white vet wrap, Fred's standard racing colors. His tongue was tied down with soft cloth, which was a standard procedure so the tongue didn't get trapped in the back of the throat and choke the horse when he was running. Some older race horses run with their tongue hanging out of the side of their mouth. The horse's tongue is very long, about twelve inches, and just flops completely loose when they run. Hanging it out the side is the horse's way of keeping his airway open, learned by experience, but it sure is ugly. Becky could see that Thunder didn't seem to mind the tongue tie.

Becky stood in the saddling paddock with her pretty hat on, nervous as could be. She was more fidgety than the horse. Fred came to stand by her. The jockey came next to stand by them. He shook Becky's hand and said he was happy to meet her. He got instructions from Fred. Keep off the rail and get him around safe. "Jockey's up" was called and there came Thunder Agard. Fred held the jockey's leg and boosted him up onto the horse. He was lead to the edge of the track where Cesar, on the pony horse, took the lead. Thunder knew Cesar and the pony horse, so he walked off with confidence. The horses paraded at a walk or trot past the grandstand while the announcer read the horse's statistics, owner, breeder, trainer, jockey, and betting odds. Bettors get a look and it's shown on television for simulcast betting at other tracks. Thunder broke into a canter. He looked cool, calm, and ready.

They galloped three fourths of the way around the track to the starting gate. The starting gate was a big, imposing, scary-looking thing, with stalls for twelve horses and a little platform for a man to stand in front of each horse. The horses approached from the back. There are gates in the front that are closed but will all spring open at once when the starter pushes a button. Doors on the back close behind each horse when it goes into a numbered stall that is just wide enough for the horse. The gate men try to get this done as rapidly as possible so that those big, athletic, nervous horses aren't trapped inside too long, getting anxious. They usually load two at a time: #1 and 6, 2 and 7, 3 and 8, 4 and 9, 5 and 10. Then "All In" was called, and the starter pushed the button to open the front gates. Loud clangs and bells sound as the horses burst out of the gate. Wound up, scared, and excited three year olds aren't very experienced, so there was sometimes bumping, pushing, or stumbling out of the gate. That's the most dangerous time of the race.

Thunder was out of the gate well. He ran in the middle of the pack, third out from the rail. All the people were yelling and screaming encouragement to their favorite. Becky was hollering instructions to the jockey, the horse, and the race in general. She was so excited, completely oblivious to everyone around her. Why yell? The jockey can't hear anything but the horse's hooves and the wind.

The announcer was calling the order of horses over the speaker. It was such a release of pent up emotions and excitement. The entire crowd was shouting for some horse by name or number. The noise was deafening. The people jumped up and down and waved their arms. That was their involvement in the race.

At the end of the turn, as the horses rounded into the straight away at the quarter mile pole, the jockey signaled Thunder Agard to give it his all by using the whip on his shoulder; three taps on the right then three taps on the left. Thunder had been trained for this in his morning workouts. Thunder leaped forward with a visible burst of speed. He was gaining, passing up to 4th, then up to 3rd. Then, the grand stand was beside him. Thunder hesitated. The jockey couldn't keep his focus. Thunder turned his head slightly to look at the crowd. His ears flicked back and forth. So much noise rushed at him. He had lost his burst of speed and momentum. He managed to cross the finish line in 5th place.

Becky was crushed. He was doing so well, gaining ground. She didn't get to be in the winner's circle. The horse got a bare minimum purse money. Bettors got zip, so his crowd was disappointed. After the race, Becky and Frank went to the barn to check out how he cooled down and how his leg was holding.

The trainer, Fred, was standing by the barn door watching the two horses on the walker. He was calm and relaxed. His western shirt was crisp, pressed jeans and boots professional, but not overdone. His tall, lean physique looked much younger than his silver hair and sun wrinkled skin indicated. As they approached, Fred stepped up to them and drawled slowly, "That was a pretty darn good first out. Clean out the gate, stayed with the pack, not afraid to run."

"Really?" Becky questioned. "You were pleased with that race?" Her lack of experience showed she had expected something else.

"Yup. Good first out. Now we know he's easily distracted by the crowd. We'll make a few changes before his next race, but that was good." Fred nodded sagely. His steady confidence was heartening. He'd run thousands. If he said it was good, then Becky believed it was good. She felt better after hearing the trainer's explanation. Of course, there is a learning curve in any sport, which she had forgotten about. Experience is the only trainer for a shouting jumping crowd like that.

Chapter 7

In racing, many commonly used terms come from Old England. The money won is called a purse because that's how it was carried and given to the winner; in a bag called a purse. Even sixth place gets enough to pay for the jockey mount fee, veterinary care that goes with racing, and a little to other expenses. The distances run is another Old English term called a furlong. A furlong is one eighth of a mile. Races are different distances, from four furlongs, or a half mile, to eight furlongs or longer. They are called one turn races or two turn races depending on how far around the track the horses run. A six-furlong race is down the straight backstretch, around one curve and down the straight home stretch. It's supposed to be easier than races of a mile or longer which have two turns to go around.

It was about a month before Thunder's conditions came up again. He had been training well and was muscled up and ready. The race was Maiden three-year-old colts and geldings, New Mexico Bred, six furlongs. It was exactly what Fred was looking for as his next race. Again, Becky was just as excited and nervous with anticipation and the hope that they could win this one. Thunder walked calmly to the saddling paddock led by his groom with whom Thunder was very familiar. He was in gate position #5 with a yellow saddle blanket. Becky stood on the #5 in the circle as owners do. The groom, a kind and gentle older Hispanic man was rubbing his head and talking to him quietly in Spanish. There was a fondness between these two that steadied the horse. His front legs were wrapped. Fred and Cesar worked together to get the saddle on and the girth tight. Then, something new was put on his head. It was white with a red "4D" in the center and little cups that come out around the back side of his eyes. Blinkers. They would keep the horse from looking backwards and sideways. Fred came to stand by Becky and noticed her staring at the blinkers.

"He's been training in them since the last race and they really help to keep him focused," Fred explained. Out came the jockey, a different one this time; hispanic, small, wiry, and very young looking. Fred said this jockey had lots of experience. The jockey shyly shook Becky's hand then turned to Fred for final instructions. "Stay off the rail, run back a little 'til the quarter pole, then drive him down the stretch."

"Jockey's up" was called and Fred legged the jockey onto Thunder. Cesar was on the pony horse to lead him in the post parade and to the gate. Cesar probably knew the horse best. He rode him most mornings and helped plan his training schedule. Cesar was certainly a man of many talents. Thunder Agard looked good in the post parade, even though he was smaller than the other Thoroughbreds.

Becky stepped inside the grand stand to watch on the TV. What a thrill to see her name as Breeder and Owner on the screen. She only had one horse on the track, not a big breeder for sure, but most people knew when her horse was running.

She wanted to get the most out of the racing experience, so she dressed up. Not church dressed up, but race track dressed up. Becky had preferred to wear skirts ever since childhood when she went to a school that had a dress code of skirts in public. Her skirt was usually flowing with either nice Cowboy boots or English boots, depending on the skirt. The hat was most important. Becky's was a big, brimmed straw hat with flowers on one side. Of course, the flowers changed to match the outfit. She loved to wear a hat and used any excuse to wear one. When people saw her at the track they smile and commented, "Your horse must be running today."

"They finished loading into the gate and they were off.

"A good break out the gate for Thunder Agard," the announcer called. Thunder was first down the center of the track. The jockey let him just run relaxed as some of the other horses pulled up beside and ahead of him on the inside rail. He was running third, about four out from the rail, most of the race. At the top of the stretch, the jockey asked for his speed. Three taps of the whip on the right shoulder then change the whip hand and four taps on the left shoulder. Thunder burst down the lane. He passed one horse. He was in second and gaining fast. The whole family was screaming "Come on you can make it!" and "Go! Go!" Becky bounced up and down like a little kid. Then there was the finish line. The race was over. He didn't win. If only it had been a little longer race maybe he could have won. "He did great," Becky exclaimed. "I am so proud of him."

After the race, back at the barn, he had cooled out well. The trainer was very satisfied. "That was OK. He was trying hard and gaining without looking all around. He's starting to get focused."

It was the first time they had seen Thunder try so hard. Frank and Becky still worried about his leg. Could it hold up to such hard racing? The fetlock was cool and solid. Thunder felt good. He was prancing and playing on the walker, looking like he'd never run a race. He was such a show off. He nickered when he saw Becky walk up to the barn.

Not a win yet, but doing better. Second pays enough for four more months of training at the track.

They didn't know when Thunder would race again. The Race Secretary looks at all the horses at the track and tries to put together ten races, with ten horses each, four days a week, that will be equally matched to entice bettors. In New Mexico, Quarter horses get four or five races a day, and Thoroughbreds get five or six a day. Half of the races must be for Fillies and Mares as they usually compete together and are not as fast as "the boys".

Anyway, the Racing Secretary has a hard job trying to please the owners, trainers, bettors, and the race track management. If a horse doesn't meet the requirements for a particular race, called conditions, he can't run in that race. Trainers tell the owner, "There's no race for your horse." It took Becky a while to understand. How can there not be a race? What do you mean none for him? There are Maiden races for horses who have never won a race. There are races for non-winners of two or three races. There are races from four and one half furlongs to a mile and a quarter, and every distance in between. There are claiming races in which a price is set before the race, and if the horse is entered in that race, any person can put a claim on him and buy him for that price. The purpose of a claiming race is to keep horses of the same level and value racing together, as well as to give every level horse a chance to win. For example, if it was a $10,000 claimer, a person would not enter a young and fast horse worth $60,000 in that race because somebody would claim him and they would lose their horse to another owner. Trainers keep an eye out for bargains in claiming races, so they are a good way to keep equal speed horses together. There are also Allowance, Handicap and Stakes races at the highest levels.

Becky couldn't keep it all straight and just had to trust the trainer to put her horse in the condition where he belonged. Frank liked to study the upcoming races on the computer to see if one was coming for Thunder.

So they didn't know when Thunder would run next until the week before, when he was entered. It could be from two weeks to six weeks or longer. When it's a long wait, it can be very frustrating. Some owners and trainers with only a few horses, like Becky, couldn't get the conditions for their horse for months. They either went broke and quit, moved to another track, or dropped down to a lower claimer. Many angry words were heard about the Racing Secretary. After Becky met him and talked to him, she realized how hard his job was to try and satisfy everyone. She understood, but was still frustrated when Thunder's conditions didn't come up.

After reviewing Thunder's performance, Fred and Cesar thought the next race should be a little longer. The familiarity of what to expect lowered the anxiety level.

Finally, after 4 weeks, Thunder got another race. Thunder came out of the middle of the gate well. He was in the lead. About 100 yards down the track, the horse to his outside came over and bumped into Thunder Agard. Three strides later Thunder bumped him back, much harder than he had been bumped. It looked like, "There, take that! You are not pushing me around."

He ran a good race and finished second. However, there was a jockey's protest because of the bump. The tape was reviewed. It was replayed on the TV what seemed like a thousand times. It was obvious to everyone that Thunder had bumped the other horse much harder than he had been hit. The first bump looked like an inexperienced horse mistake. Thunder's bump looked like calculated retaliation by the horse. The jockey hadn't expected or caused the bump. Luckily, no one was hurt. What could be said? Thunder was disqualified from second down to third place behind the horse he bumped. Oh well, that's horse racing. Thunder did have spunk.

Chapter 8

Another frustration came up. They had three races and no wins with three different jockeys. Part of the problem seemed to be that the jockeys didn't know how to ride Thunder or what he could do. Becky was frustrated by the lack of control and knowledge of the jockeys. She wondered why they didn't get the same jockey every time.

Jockeys must make a living and it's an in creditably hard job. They should be brave, strong, smart and small. They get hooked on the adrenaline rush of each race. Some jockeys ride in several races a day. That's a lot to keep together all the time.

Becky learned the trainers had to deal with jockey agents. Jockeys had agents? She had never thought of. Some people told her they were blood sucking leaches. Others said they were the ones that controlled the track. Most said jockeys couldn't ride without them. Becky had never seen or met a jockey agent, and she didn't see anyone around that looked like an agent. Apparently, the agents study the entries as soon as they come out, which is 7-10 days before the race date. They try to find their jockey the best chance to ride a winning horse because they only get paid a percentage of the jockey's winnings, and the jockey only gets paid a percentage of the horse's winnings. Jockeys get paid a small mount fee, but their real earnings are 10% of the horse's winnings. They and their agents want them to win. Therefore, the best horses get the best jockeys, and the trainers with the most winning horses gets first choice. It becomes a cycle that is hard for a newcomer to break into. New or beginner jockeys have to ride lesser known horses and try to build up their reputations, and beginner horses get the newer jockeys. Catch 22. The trainer's reputation has a lot of influence also.

Becky's trainer had a good reputation and usually got a good jockey, just not the same one so far.

Some jockeys are young kids. Some kids don't have a strong sense of responsibility. One called Fred just hours before a race to say he couldn't make it that day to ride. That left Fred scrambling for a jockey for Thunder at the last minute, choosing from those who didn't already have a mount in that race. It was a jockey who had never even ridden him in morning workouts. Fred was angry and Becky could tell he was embarrassed by the situation, but he didn't say anything. His stern silence spoke volumes. He just made a mental note and that jockey never rode for him again.

Some jockeys have trouble making the light weight, especially as they get older. Some use all sorts of methods to lose weight; dieting, running, sweat boxes, and occasionally pills. A few jockeys have drinking or drug habits that make them undependable, but those are the minority. Some jockeys are given days off for unsportsmanlike behavior, so they can't ride in races for a certain number of days. Becky didn't know what unsportsmanlike behavior was until she saw one jockey hit another jockey with his whip pretending to use it for his own horse.

Some get days off for excessively aggressive riding, but aren't they supposed to ride aggressively? Who has the say over that? The racing Stewards have the say.

So jockeys are the key to a racehorse's success. Becky pondered and studied the jockey situation. She never had spoken personally to a jockey. The trainer always set the ride up. There didn't seem to be any social interaction between owners and jockeys that Becky knew about.

Becky could see the problem but had no control over it. She was not a person who is comfortable with no control. She studied the options. When visiting Paraguay a couple years before, she had seen a young boy, not over twelve years old, dressed in boots and carrying a short whip and helmet get on the bus and get off at the race track. They must have rules, but starting young wasn't one of them.

One day at the track, Becky confronted her trainer: "Fred, why can't we just go to South America and get our own personal jockey?" She was serious. It seemed like a good solution to her. He or she could apprentice for Fred, then get licensed in the US. Fred didn't think it was very funny or even possible.

"We'll get this figured out," he stated flatly but firmly. That was his only comment. He didn't understand Becky's frustration.

Becky's anxiety over not being able to control who the jockey was made her more and more stressed and grumpy.

Thunder Agard's next race was in Albuquerque and was a little different. It was seven and one half furlongs, with the same conditions as before, but with a different jockey. This jockey had worked Thunder a couple mornings, so he was riding knowing the horse a little bit. He told Cesar, "I like the feel of this horse and we can get along." Becky hoped he was the right one for her horse. Fourth time's the charm.

Becky's new red and black hat, with its wide brim, feathers, and long quills, was picked just for the winner's circle. She stood in the saddling paddock. The wind was blowing sharply, so Becky had one hand on her skirt and one hand on her hat. They had gotten the #2 gate position. He was by far the smallest horse in the race at 15.2 hands and sucked up like a marathon runner.

Fred gave the new jockey instructions. "Don't hang on the rail. Don't get dirt in his face, and stay out a little. Wait 'til the Stretch, then push him as hard as you can." Same instructions, different jockey. The jockey came to shake Becky's hand, smiled, and was legged up onto Thunder. This jockey was tall and lanky.

Thunder broke well, but was on the rail. Coming out of the #2 hole, the rail is just right there. Thunder was running first but two other horses pulled ahead on the outside and he dropped back to fourth or fifth, still lapped with the pack. He was getting boxed in on the back stretch with horses in front, to the side, and behind him. Becky started yelling at the jockey–not that he could hear, thank goodness, but the universal energy of yelling instructions out loud seemed to have some effect. It helped Becky at least. "Get out. Start angling out now. Get off the rail NOW." Then at the center of the turn, she started shouting "Start now. Go now. Don't wait until it's too late."

The jockey did angle out off the rail, but stayed back and didn't push. He floated wide on the turn to about four wide and gave Thunder the whip; a few taps on the right shoulder, changed hands and a few taps on the left. Thunder changed leads and shifted into another gear. He flew past the two horses closest to him. He was third and gaining, passed the second horse and still gaining. Pulling away, he crossed the finish line alone in the lead. Glistening, nostrils flared and ears up, he looked so happy.

Becky buzzed with excitement. "We won. We won! Let's get to the winner's circle. Where's my hat? Oh, it's on my head." It was Becky's first time in the winner's circle for the picture she had been waiting for so long. She tried to get everyone lined up like she wanted. "You move over here. I'll stand by Thunder. Closer together, hurry!" she called to her husband and friends. There was only a short time to get a hot sweaty horse to stand still. The jockey was still mounted. Fred and Cesar stood at the horse's rear. The groom held the horse's Head, and Becky, Frank, family, and friends lined up in front of the horse's head.

It was over so fast. Thunder was off to the test barn where all winners go. The jockey was off to get his next mount. The bettors were off to see what they won. Becky was still standing there amazed. Success at last! This is what she wanted, a winer's picture.

The whole family and their friends went out to dinner. There were twenty of them, so they took over one corner of the restaurant. Everyone talked all at once. The burst of speed was exciting. The win picture was passed around and admired. Even other restaurant patrons got to see the picture. Thunder had all four feet off the ground. Becky's red cheeks and giant smile matched her hat.

Win pictures are a unique art form. They have all the pertinent information: Race #, race date, track, trainer, owner and jockey's names, and the names of the winning horse, the second-place horse, and the third-place horse. There is also a picture as the horse crosses the finish line, along with the winner's circle picture with the jockey, trainer, groom, and all the family and friends. Sometimes they also add a small picture from the post parade. It's all printed in bright color on an 8X10 glossy photo, ready in one hour. It's amazing.

The photographers who create them are masters at what they do. They know how to get everyone lined up for the perfect shot in a short time frame. The "Win Picture" is a permanent memory that can be hung on the wall or shown to everyone.

Thunder's picture was by Coady Photography.

Chapter 9

The Albuquerque race meet was finished for the year. The hard work of moving about 1,500 horses to a new track began. The grooms had to pack up all the saddles, bridles, buckets, leg wraps, blinkers, grooming tools, and everything else used, to be moved to the next race track. Most were going to Hobbs, New Mexico on the Texas border to the Zia Racetrack and Casino. Everything was loaded into trucks and horse trailers. Feed and bedding were hauled to the new track or purchased there. The trainers usually hauled five to eight horses at a time in their long gooseneck trailers. Some professional haulers with big vans made multiple trips full of horses to get them to the next race meet. Most of the people on the back side, where the horses are kept and the grooms, trainers and riders do all their work, have done this so often it is old hat for them. All the people working on the backside said it's one of the hardest parts of track life.

Some take their families with them while others leave their families at a home base and make the trip alone. Most are older with no children, but some have their teenage children working with them, and a few have small children that stay at the track with their parents.

Most of the grooms and trainers are second or third generation race horse people. Becky laughed as she watched two men dissemble and fold up a walker to put on the back of a flatbed trailer until she saw the forklift guy show up and put the walker on the trailer with two others. It looked like major chaos, but within three days everything was gone. Gone. Everything, even the stall gates, were removed and went to the next track. The barns were raked clean and shut up until next year. This moving was quite impressive and very hard work, but part of racetrack life.

Zia was a newer race track that was built all at once from scratch. It had nice, orderly matching barns with roads in between them that drained well. The stalls were large and airy so the horses seemed content. The saddling paddock was easy for spectators and owners to see. They had a nice comfortable Jockey's Club to view the races from. Many people came for lunch and stayed all afternoon. The food was good, the drinks were good, and the view was good. The betting cashiers were convenient both on the track level and upstairs. There were televisions all over with simulcast races, so bettors could place bets all over the country. The small casino was filled with slot machines.

Gamblers have changed. They like the slots–simple, mindless, and not influenced by outside forces. Without the casinos, racing would collapse. To be allowed to have a casino, they are required to hold races a certain number of days per year with a percentage of the casino money going to purses of the races. Most New Mexico tracks raced four days a week, three or four months out of the year. Betting on racehorses is complicated and slower than other forms of gambling. Becky was not a risk taker at all and usually didn't bet, but she loved to study the bloodlines, speed index, past races, trainer's record, and jockey's record to make an educated guess. Racing gives bettors a sense of control over their choice, but it's still a horse race and anything can happen.

Becky and Frank both agreed that they were thankful the law required live horse racing for a "Racino" so that the next generation could experience something that they enjoyed so much. That's why they included their children and grandchildren whenever possible.

Thunder Agard settled into his new location. Fred phoned, "It's time to step him up in class and run for bigger purses with faster horses. I have a kid riding him who really seems to get the best out of him." With his years of experience, Fred knew what he was doing, but he was rather reserved and didn't build horses up to the owner. In fact, it was rare that he called at all, so Frank usually called him to find out what was going on. Most information was on the computer about entries and race schedules, but Fred hadn't moved to the computer age.

"Thank Heavens. Maybe if we have the same jockey for a few races in a row, at least one variable will be eliminated," Frank replied. "When will he run again?"

"Soon," Fred drawled. "I'm looking for a race. This is where he needs to be."

All of the races were learning experiences for Thunder and his owners. His next race was proof of that. As Becky and Frank watched anxiously, Thunder was loaded into the #1 gate, closest to the rail. As all the horses broke well out of the gate, Thunder was boxed in with horses in front of him, horses beside him, and horses behind him. He had to run the same pace as the others because there was nowhere to go. He ate dirt most of the way. About two thirds through the race, with no opening in sight, the jockey decided to try slowing down to find an opening to go around the outside. Thunder slowed down then just gave up. He finished 12 lengths off the winning horse. Becky felt so bad for Thunder. She wasn't jumping up and down and yelling, just concentrated on watching her horse. It didn't matter to her if he won or not but Thunder seemed dejected as he crossed the finish line. He had dirt all over his face, chest, and front legs. He didn't do his usual pep step prancing back to the barn.

Thunder looked annoyed at the other horses. He flattened his ears as they passed. Becky knew horses don't reason like humans, or dwell on things, but she could see disappointment in Thunder's eyes in that moment. He hadn't gotten the chance to run the way he wanted. The resilient racetrack people just say, "That's why it's called horse racing. He'll live to run another day." It's that faith that kept Becky wanting to give him another chance.

Thunder was running well and getting better each time. He won two races at Zia before moving to Sunland Park, a beautiful track in southern New Mexico near El Paso Texas. Becky was really excited to go see him race there. He was running in a race on Saturday, but they arrived on Friday night and stayed over in a nice hotel. This track accommodated the owners with free box seats in the Clubhouse, good food and drinks, and nice big TV's. Since it was winter time, Becky decided she could wear her felt hat even though the weather was warm. She had on a black Zorro hat with gold sparkly Christmas holly, black boots, and a bronze colored broomstick skirt. Smiling and nodding to everyone, she was feeling and looking great. Age seemed to vanish as she moved around the track when her horse was running. Everyone called him "her horse" as if Frank had nothing to do with it, because he stayed quietly in the background just enjoying seeing his wife so excited and happy. He would do almost anything to make her happy and she knew it and loved him for it.

The race was a $20,000 claimer optional, but Fred said not to worry because nobody would claim an older gelding with an old fracture. Everyone on the backside, trainers, grooms and riders knew all the horses and how they usually went. Not worry! Becky became anxious when she realized it was a claiming race. Someone may see his potential and claim him. What if someone did claim him? Was she ready to let him go? No, she was having so much fun with racing and he was a very special horse to her.

"I don't really want to lose him," She spoke quietly to the trainer.

"He needs a race and this is all that's available for his conditions now. Even if they claim him and he wins, you get
$20,000 and 60% of $20,000, plus someone else will be paying his expense," deadpanned Fred. He never seemed to be attached to a particular horse after working with so many for so many years. This was his business.

"Ok, I'll try to look at it that way, but I really don't want someone else to have him." Becky had raised him from a baby. She had chosen his father and mother. However, that was the race he was in and the handicappers had picked him to be on the board. That meant he probably would be one of the top three. Our best jockey was on another horse in this race, so Fred had selected an older jockey with a good reputation and years of experience. He had ridden for our trainer before. Becky had heard of him. He had won quite a few races. He should be good on Thunder.

The horses all came to the paddock; a chestnut, a grey, and five browns. The excitement began to build. Becky was standing on the number in the saddling paddock. After Thunder was all tacked up, Fred came to stand by her. The jockey came out and shook her hand. "Glad to meet you ma'am." He smiled broadly. He was a very polite, small, muscular older man weathered by the sun. He got final instructions and then "Jockeys Up" was called.

Good break. Everyone came out of the gate evenly. The horses started to line out about 100 yards from the gate with Thunder in the back. That was OK, not against the rail and he liked to come from the back. Down the back stretch he was losing ground and by the turn he was 13 lengths behind the others and just galloping. Why? Oh, my gosh! He must be hurt. Becky's stomach twisted into a hard knot and her mouth went as dry as cotton balls. She just stood and watched, holding her breath. That leg must have reinjured. Fred said it wouldn't last forever and this was his twelfth race. Becky hoped he made it off the track. She hurried down to the rail to watch him pass. He finished last, 24 lengths off the lead.

That was way behind. He didn't look hurt. He wasn't bleeding from the nose or limping. Becky hurried toward the barn, but dress boots were not made for rapid cross country travel. Tears were forming in her eyes and her smile quivered. Her husband met her at the bleachers and took her hand. "Don't worry honey. We can still take him home." It seemed to take them forever to get to his barn.

By the time Becky got to the barn, she was worked up into a tizzy. Her ears were ringing. Anxiety twisted her belly. She was squeezing Frank's hand so hard he flinched. She rounded the corner and there he was, all washed up and on the walker. Thunder nickered when he saw her then reared and bucked a little while prancing on the walker. What the hell? Becky crumbled like a popped balloon and leaned against Frank who stood solidly beside her. All the anxiety rushed out of her and nothing else was left. Relief flooded through her and she felt limp as an overcooked noodle.

Where was everybody? Where was our trainer? What had happened? Only the older Hispanic groom stood watching the horse on the walker. He had always been Thunder's groom and seemed fond of him, but he didn't say anything; just nodded and continued his work.

Frank felt the leg all over and the other legs also. He seemed perfectly fine; not tired or blowing hard at all. They moved back to the grandstand to wait until the race day was finished to talk to their trainer. He had been down giving the jockey what for. Becky didn't hear it, but was told by others it was quite a butt chewing. When Frank approached Fred, he was calm and stoic, like he usually was. Fred could see Becky was quite upset and couldn't talk. "Your horse isn't hurt. He isn't even tired. That was just a workout for him. The jockey froze coming out of the gate. Didn't trust the horse and didn't ride him."

Everyone on the back side wondered why Thunder Agard came in last by 24 lengths. It's a very small, gossipy group. Becky heard that after years of riding, certain horses or situations just cause a fear reaction in the jockey occasionally. This was hard on the jockey's reputation. One trainer friend even joked, "I'm sure glad I didn't claim your horse." At least Becky's fears were relieved. As they say at the track, "That's horse racing. He'll live to race another day." But Becky vowed not to ever put him in another Claiming Race. It was so hard on her nerves.

Apparently, Thunder was not an easy horse to ride. It seemed that the jockey strongly influenced his racing ability. That made jockey selection one of the most important factors for Thunder.

Chapter 10

Thunder turned five years old on January first, as all Thoroughbreds do, even though his birthday was in mid-April. He was now in the category of older race horses. His career started late. He didn't race as a two-year-old and didn't start racing until the fall of his three-year-old year. He ran well as a four-year-old just learning the game. Now he was starting his five-year-old year with a sound mind and body. He enjoyed racing and was full of confidence.

He had started to play cute tricks that annoyed the grooms and riders. Because he was so confident, he could get away with them. When he galloped in the morning, Thunder loved being out on the track with all the other horses, running and getting lots of attention. When he'd finished, he didn't want to leave and go back to his barn. He would start toward his barn then walk sideways and act like he didn't know how to rein as he wandered all over the barn area. One morning, the rider, who wasn't paying attention, ended up several barns away from where he was going when Thunder stopped suddenly in front of a different barn. Becky had seen riding horses do the same thing when they wanted to go a different direction than the rider. Of course, the grooms and riders have other horses to work and didn't have time to play around. The quick solution was to have a pony horse meet him coming off the track and lead him to his own groom and barn. The long solution was a good spat on the butt. Thunder was such a funny boy. He finally got his good spanking and straightening up from Cesar.

Mornings at the track start early. Someone is there at each barn around 4:30 AM to start preparations to feed. Almost all the approximately one hundred trainers have had the same barns for years; and the same number of horses, give or take a few. When one horse eats, they all want to eat, so it's standard that everyone starts around 5:00 to feed. It was hard for Becky to even think at that time in the morning, so she was glad it wasn't her job. She was definitely not a morning person, and seldom got to the track to see Thunder's early morning workouts.

The grooms feed, clean, and get the day started. Almost all the approximately 1,400 horses at the track are ridden five days a week, except when they race. Some are walked or ponied instead. It's the trainer's and assistant trainer's job to keep the schedule and know which horse needs what kind of work each day. The track opens for riding from 5:30 to 8:00, and there will be as many horses out at one time as there are riders to take them out. Some morning riders are old jockeys. Some want to be jockeys. Some were jockeys who got too big. Some are just very good riders who like the work. Several girls get to do morning workouts, and a few go on to be jockeys. It's a hard job physically and mentally. If they can impress a trainer, he can support the rider and give them a chance to ride their horses in races so they can get started as a new jockey.

The track takes a break from 8:00 to 8:30 to run the tractors around and get the surface back into shape. With that many horses galloping over the dirt/clay/sand, it gets packed, shifts, or gets slick spots, so it needs to be harrowed before the second group of horses starts working. The track is closed from 10:30 until race time. The tractor boys are out before every race as well as between races to keep the surface as smooth and even as possible. There is a water truck in New Mexico that sprinkles the track every morning and between races. Dust could cause serious respiratory problems for the horses and riders, so it's kept slightly damp all the time. The water truck passed through the barn area a few times a day as well.

There is one person who is well versed in race track composition that monitors the hardness, cuppiness, and stickiness. He adds sand, clay, or composite. The track is watered, harrowed, smoothed, and fine harrowed between each race as well as during workout breaks in the mornings. Riders or trainers tell the track groundskeeper if they think there is a problem, and where, so it can be examined. If several injuries happen in the same day, the track surface is examined closely for stickiness, looseness, or hardness even though it's not usually the fault of the track surface. With the advent of synthetic tracks that have rubber and sand over a solid footing, the horses must get used to that surface in order to run well. The same is true of horses that run on turf (grass). Luckily, New Mexico has neither of those surfaces. Some horses run naturally in the mud, and in the East, rain doesn't stop very many races. In New Mexico, some of our horses have never seen rain or a muddy track.

Many people work so hard on the backside of the track from 4:30 AM to 10:30 AM. They are mostly Hispanic, and are often multi-generation families who have worked on the racetrack. They feed the horses, clean the stalls and walkways, tack and untack horses for the riders, show the horses to the veterinarian for inspection, hose off and cool out the horses coming back from a ride, and wash leg wraps and saddle pads. If a person came to visit the barn at 11:00 AM, they would think these are lazy people because they are all resting and eating lunch. They don't realize that is because they have been very busy and done a full day's work already. If the trainer has a horse racing that day, it starts all over again two hours before the race. If they don't have an entry, it starts all over again at 4:00 PM with feeding, watering, cleaning, and preparation for tomorrow. Becky came to admire how hard the people on the backside (in the barn area) worked with little recognition. Most of them do it for the love of working with horses. It darn sure is not for the money because none of them were rich. They are the lowest rung, but they have a great deal of influence over the horses as they spent more time with them than anyone.

Chapter 11

Frank was excited about having a horse on the track. He studied the statistics listed on Equibase, a website all about racing. It included information on the horses, jockeys, trainers, and owners.

"Honey, do you know what Thunder's speed index is?" Frank asked as he sat back in his recliner looking at his Ipad.

"No, I have no idea what a speed index even is or what our horse's is," Becky sighed in exasperation. She didn't spend much time on a computer unless forced to for work, and never for pleasure. Frank continued reading his Ipad, totally caught up in looking at the statistics.

"Well, are you going to tell me or not?" Becky huffed.

"I thought you said you weren't interested in that stuff. Anyway, it's the number that tells how fast his time in the race was. It's used by handicappers and bettors to predict who should win a race. The higher the number the better. Thunder's is 85. I think that is good." Frank grinned as he told Becky. He was proud to be something she didn't know. She always seemed to know quite a bit about most things, but not so much about numbers. In the computer is a record of all of Thunder's races, his placing, his money earned year by year, his winnings per start, and his rank in the United States with other race horses. As Frank studied the numbers, he felt better and better about their race horse.

"Honey, did you ever dream we'd have a race horse?" Frank mused.

"Yes dear, but this is so much better than I dreamed. Hundreds of people breed race horses and never get a winner. Most are never as good as he is already. He may get even better yet."

"We are sure having fun with this, aren't we?"

"This is the most fun we've had with a horse since the kids stopped showing. I've learned so much and experienced more ups and downs in one year than I ever expected," Becky mused.

The summer of 2014, Thunder Agard, a five-year-old, was running at SunRay Park in Farmington, NM. It was the next track on the rotation around the state. This track is called a "bull ring" because it's not a full mile around the circle. It is only six furlongs, so the turns are tighter. Some mile races start on the long extension of the home stretch so the horses go past the grandstand twice to the finish line. That is exciting for the spectators and bettor. It was the perfect track for Thunder because his early training in Utah was on a bull ring. He was smaller than most thoroughbreds, so it was easier for him to corner, and most races have two turns. Becky and Frank liked the track as owners because it was small and well organized with the saddling paddock and winner's circle convenient to get to. The Jockey Club seating was free to owners, the food and drinks were good, and the casino was small and out of the way of the racing area. It was close enough to home so that many friends could come to watch Thunder's races. It was a long way to the backside, so Becky learned the hard way to wear comfortable boots if she planned on making that trip.

Thunder's first race at Sunray was with a tough class of horses. He was picked by the handicappers for third place. The jockey Fred picked had never ridden Thunder in a race, but had ridden him in morning workouts, so he said he felt comfortable with him. Becky was NOT comfortable with yet another new jockey. She asked other owners, trainers, and race track people about him. They said, "This jockey needs the win." One man said, "He'll ride the hair off a dog." In horse racing, a lazy horse is called a dog, so that means that if there is anything at all in the horse, this jockey can get it out of him. Becky loved the sound of that.

In the saddling paddock, Thunder was a perfect gentleman, tacked up, blinkers on, but something looked different. He had no front leg wraps; no red and white from the fetlock up the cannon bone to the knee. Becky wondered why, but had to ask later because at that moment, the jockey came out. Fred gave the same instructions to the letter. The jockey shook Becky's hand and said confidently, "I'll give it my best ma'am."

The horses all had a clean break from the gate. Thunder was running middle of the pack on the outside. At the end of the final turn, the jockey pushed Thunder. Tap-tap-tap with the whip; changed hands and used the whip again. That was Thunder's signal and he burst into extra speed, passing the other horses. Everyone was screaming and jumping. "Go Thunder! Come on boy." Tap and whoosh. The jockey was just waving his whip and Thunder continued to accelerate. The announcer called, "Winner going away by five lengths, Thunder Agard."

Down to the winner's circle we all hustled. The win picture was Becky's favorite part. Many friends had come to see him run, and they all came to the winner's circle. Frank got to be in the picture, but he stood behind all the ladies and could barely be seen. The odds were twenty to one due to his previous loss by a good distance, so Becky's friends who made bets were all happy and proud. Win pictures were ordered for everyone in the picture– a permanent memory of the day.

As the friends headed elsewhere, Frank and Becky went to the back side to check on their horse. Frank stopped at the test barn. When a horse wins a race, he goes straight to the test barn where he gives a urine sample which is tested for drugs, stimulants, depressants, pain killers, vasodilators, respiratory dilators, or steroids. The horses arrive at the test barn tired and thirsty. The groom walked him in a circle and gave him drinks from his own bucket every five minutes. At forty-five minutes, they are led into a bedded stall where a person with a cup on a stick waits. He whistles softly and the horse usually relaxes and pees right away. If the horse doesn't pee, they keep walking and drinking for up to ninety minutes, then a blood sample is drawn. Samples are divided. One for the lab for immediate testing and one is kept frozen to retest if there is a positive test or a protest. A veterinarian supervises all this. He is responsible for getting all the samples properly labeled, shipped, and stored. Because lots of money is involved, it is very important the right horse is identified by tattoo number, the sample is correctly labeled, and all times and procedures are followed exactly.

Thunder did well. He walked, drank, peed, and headed back to his stall. Becky never worried about a positive test because she had full trust in their trainer. The paperwork or testing methods can be done incorrectly but very seldom is. Many people want to think all these horses are on some performance enhancing dangerous drugs. However, a miniscule number of Thoroughbreds take anything but furosemide or Lasix, a legal medication to prevent rupture of the capillaries in the nasal cavity when a horse breathes heavily. Furosemide is more necessary in very dry climates because the membranes dry out and are fragile. Even people get nose bleeds when it's so dry and they exercise heavily.

Becky met with Cesar back at the stall where Thunder had already been washed and was on the walker. Cesar greeted her warmly with a big smile on his face. He was pleased when one of his horses won. She asked why Thunder wasn't wearing front leg wraps like he had been in the past.

Cesar explained, "I usually ride him in the mornings, and I noticed last week when we went to the track, from the time we left the barn 'til we got to the track, he moved like his legs hurt and he didn't want to go onto the track. That was very unusual for him. He normally is rushing to get out in the mornings. I turned around and rode back to the barn, untacked him, and removed the leg wraps. I put him on the walker and he bucked and played, showing no signs of lameness or pain whatsoever. I decided to tack him back up and go to the track again because he needed the work. I left the front leg wraps off. He galloped fine and eager, coming back sound and happy. After discussing it with Fred, we decided maybe the wraps were putting pressure on the old fracture. We thought we'd try to run him without leg wraps." He grinned broadly, proud of the results. Becky could see how observant Ceasar was and how much he liked Thunder.

Thunder had just run his best race without leg wraps. It all came down to being familiar with the horse and listening to what the horse wanted to do his best. Cesar was a very good observer and listener. Becky thought he would become a very good trainer one day as he was getting experience under one of the best older trainers around. He had sure helped explain the racing game to them. His wife also had a trainer's license, and it was their dream to someday have their own training barn together. She was working as a veterinary assistant, gaining valuable knowledge for their future when they could start their own training operation. With so many trainers getting old, Becky was thrilled to see young people learning and wanting to continue this tradition.

Three weeks later, the same conditions came up again: seven and a half furlongs, NM bred colts and geldings, three years and up. That's Thunder, so Fred entered him again. He drew a different starting gate position. A different jockey was riding him. Becky had no idea why they didn't have the same jockey. She liked him and he had done such a good job. The trainer knows the jockeys and agents, and this jockey had a good reputation and was one of Fred's favorite riders. The race ran almost the same. Thunder Agard burst down the final stretch with very little pushing and won by lengths. Becky was so excited as she rushed down to the winner's circle. She was sporting a new fancy tan felt hat with cloth roses and feathers, a beige broomstick skirt, and boots that she wore just in case they got a win photo.

Becky didn't bet on her horse. She felt that the win was enough. She didn't think she was a gambler and couldn't stand to lose. However, this made Frank laugh because everything she did in life was a gamble. Becky took lots of chances that he wouldn't dare. She was always pushing the edge a little just to see where it was. The odds were low because of his last win, so the bettors didn't make much money. That's how it works. This win picture looked just like the last one. Thunder was the only horse in the picture and all four feet were off the ground. Only the color of the saddle blanket and the hat Becky was wearing were different.

The SunRay meet was over in mid-July. Everyone packed up and moved all the equipment and horses, and the track closed down until the next year. Thunder moved to Ruidoso Downs. It is one of the most famous race tracks because of the million dollar All American Futurity for Quarter Horses, and for the beautiful mountain resort town surrounding it. It is also a bull ring track for Thoroughbreds with a wide straight Quarter Horse track closest to the bleachers. Quarter Horse races are more numerous than Thoroughbred races in Ruidoso.

Becky was not fond of Ruidoso Downs. The saddling paddock is in the infield and not convenient for the owners to see their horses. They had to pass under both tracks through a long tunnel to get there and back. The barns were old and scattered with poor drainage and no place to park. Their clubhouse was expensive and so was the food and drinks. They assumed that if people had a race horse, then they had lots of money, and were there to spend it in Ruidoso.

The town is beautiful, surrounded by mountains. It's full of art galleries and museums. The McGary Foundry makes larger than life bronze statues of horses and Indians. It takes at least three days just to visit all the exciting shops and galleries. The Apache "Inn of the Mountain Gods" resort and golf course are nearby. The mountain near the track was recovering from a devastating forest fire that came right down to the edge of the racetrack parking lot. It was a close call, but didn't damage any of the grandstand, track, or barns. It has a small casino called the "Billy the Kid" casino, so it's a Racino.

Despite all that, it was a good place for Thunder to run because of the tight turns and length of the races.

When his conditions came up, Thunder was entered. The trainer got the same jockey as the last race. He was becoming Becky's favorite jockey since he had ridden Thunder four times in races before at Sunray with good results.

Thunder was good out the gate and holding fourth place down the backstretch, but was trapped against the rail. There was no place to move out. No horse was fast enough nor slow enough to make a gap. Thunder tired on the rail and hated to run with mud kicked in his face. He placed fourth as the tight pack didn't change places. After the race, the jockey was disappointed in the ride and apologized. "I won't let that happen to him again. That's where he broke and I thought the other horses would make a gap, but they didn't." The jockey didn't have to say anything, but it was nice of him. Becky saw exactly what had happened. It had rained all day the day before and the track was sticky and deep. July to September is the rainy season in New Mexico and always unpredictable. As she had learned, "Oh well, it's a horse race. He'll live to run another day."

About three weeks later, the same conditions came up and Thunder was in another race. This time, he drew the outside post position. Becky's favorite jockey was on board again. It was most of the same group of horses he had been running against before.

Fred only told the jockey, "You know what he can do. Don't get trapped."Thunder won going away, again the only horse in the finish photo. Becky and Frank could not be there for the win picture as the rest of life had gotten in the way. The trainer's wife and her friend stood in the photo with the groom, Cesar, and Fred. Often, it was only one week's notice before Thunder ran, so it was hard to be at all the races–especially when they were far from home. Thank goodness for Equibase and "Horse Racing Now" apps where they could watch the race on the computer. Often, Frank watched the race over and over, analyzing every step. He showed it to anybody who seemed interested. It was quite informative and fun, both the wins and the losses.

Some losses were horse error. Some losses were jockey error. Sometimes Thunder was just outrun by faster horses, and sometimes it was just luck.

The Quarter Horse All American started, and all the Thoroughbreds were moved to Albuquerque. Thunder didn't have a race for a while, so he got a little rest and training to stay in shape.

Chapter 12

One morning, Fred called with a rather big announcement. That was unusual. We usually had to call him about the races and he didn't communicate much." Because of his wins this year, Thunder Agard qualified to be nominated for the New Mexico Lineage Classic Stakes race," he said. It was a very prestigious race for the top New Mexico colts and geldings four years old and up for the distance of a mile and 1/16.

"There was a nomination fee, but I went ahead and nominated him. We won't know for two weeks who will be in the race, but there is no reason he shouldn't be in there." He didn't ask if we wanted to enter, he just went ahead and put him in. Fred knew we trusted his judgment. "Then there is a gate fee if he is accepted. It's the best of the best in New Mexico, and we are one of them." It was the first-time Becky had heard Fred sound excited about what this horse could do. And he had used "we", including everyone involved with Thunder. Fred was usually very low key and noncommittal so that owners wouldn't be over confident then disappointed if it didn't happen.

Frank knew they wouldn't announce the selections for another ten days, but he checked the computer daily to see who had been nominated and where we ranked with them. Would Fred be able to get their favorite jockey if other top trainers had horses in the race? Who would the jockey choose to ride? Worry, excitement, and anticipation all built. The thrill was worth it. Becky could always hope for a win.

Finally, the horses were chosen and announced. Thunder Agard was one of eight in the Stakes Race for one mile, and a sixteenth with a purse of $60,000 plus a trophy for the owner, trainer, and jockey. That would be the longest distance Thunder had ever been asked to race, but he was training well so the slightly longer distance shouldn't bother him. Becky was so excited. she told herself several times a day, "We're in." She called all her family and friends to tell them about the race. The kids started getting excited and planning to all be there for the big day.

"Honey, I think you need to tone it down a little. This is a horse race you remember," Frank cautioned. He thought there might be a big disappointment if she built it up too high. She didn't care if they won or lost. Being in this company with all the hoopla was all the excitement she needed. The race was in Albuquerque, so everyone could come because it was close to home. One son was coming from Utah. One daughter was coming back from Kansas with several grandchildren in hopes of getting there in time for the race. Frank's best friend and his wife were planning to accompany them for the weekend.

Becky and Frank received an invitation for a luncheon party for all the Lineage race entrants. There were five Quarter Horse races and six Thoroughbred races divided by age and gender. It was so nice to get a fancy printed invitation to a party. Becky stewed for days over what to wear. She wanted to fit in with the other race horse owners, not over or under dressed. This was her first event with racehorse owners, trainers, and track officials. She didn't know who to ask or how they usually dressed. She decided on boots, of course, and a hat, but not a big race day hat. This was an afternoon luncheon, so a small conservative hat would be good. Becky preferred skirts, but she knew nobody else would be in one, so she chose pants. She tried on six pairs before one suited her just right. A nice denim and lace blouse finished off the outfit with a small straw hat with a feather and hat pin. Of course, Frank, like most men, hadn't given a thought about what to wear. He would just take whatever was in the closet that day. It would be standard Wrangler jeans, a long-sleeved cotton shirt, and boots with his good cowboy hat. Almost all the men would be dressed alike; except for the poor race track officials who had to be in suits.

The luncheon, held at the Down of Albuquerque, had flowers on the tables and huge posters of each race with the post position blank. Silver trophy cups lined the tables in front of the posters. Each horse's name was called and placed in its post position as they read the breeder, owner, trainer, and jockey information. The feeling of having her horse's name called gave Becky tingles starting at the top of her head and going all the way down her back. It was all she could do not to stand up and cheer. She thought of Grandpa Agard, who was probably jumping up and down in Heaven. The feeling was pleasant and satisfying. She thought, "I did that. I picked his dam and sire and raised him." It's like a mommy seeing her child's name in the school Christmas Program.

The President of the NM Horseman's Association and the Race Secretary, along with the officials of the racetrack, were all there. There were people from the press present. Fred's wife had been instrumental in starting the New Mexico Bred program, and she had a Quarter Horse running in the Lineage. It was odd that they weren't there. It made Becky wonder why and she had an odd feeling.

Becky walked by the trophies all lined up and read the engraving on the one for the owner of the winner of their race. Wow, she wanted that trophy like a kid who wants a new bike. It was shiny. The likelihood of that happening was small, but who knew. That was what all the build up to this race day was for. Everyone had high hopes. Frank was getting excited, but trying not to show it. They never in their wildest dreams thought they'd have a horse of this caliber in this kind of race. Some of the people in the room have had fifty or more race horses and this was their first time, too. Becky's husband was good with people and remembered names and faces. He pointed them out to Becky, greeting and talking to them as they mingled around the room. Becky could only smile and see their happy faces smiling back. She couldn't remember their names one hour later. She remembered horses better. She knew which ones Thunder had outrun, which ones had outrun him, and which ones they had never run against. She could drive down the highway and see a horse standing in a field and remember that four years ago they had treated him for a foot laceration, or recognize a colt that was attacked by dogs last year, but wouldn't recognize the owner. Frank doesn't even question her memory for horses after all these years. That's why they were a good team. He's the people person for her and she was the details person for him.

They left the luncheon elated. They were in the #2 post position. It wasn't the best for Thunder, but the race was long so he'd have lots of time to find his position. There were only seven in the race now. When Becky got home, she was talking to her friend whose dad was a racehorse trainer. She mentioned she was surprised not to see Fred and his wife at the luncheon.

"Oh, didn't you hear? His wife died on Thursday night," her friend said.

Becky was shocked and could hardly believe it. It felt like a kick in the belly. "I just saw her last month. She was in my win picture at Ruidoso when we couldn't make it. She taught me a lot about the racing ups and downs. What happened?"

"I don't know. Dad didn't say, but it seemed kind of sudden. I'll let you know when my dad finds out."

"I am so sorry," Becky's lip twitched. "Do you think it will affect us racing next Saturday?" She felt a little callous thinking about her race, but she couldn't help it.

"No, the assistant trainer will take over. That's what assistant trainers are for. That's what happened when my Dad was in the hospital. The assistant trainers are qualified to do it all," her friend reassured her sympathetically.

"Oh, good. Cesar has been with Thunder from the beginning and knows him well. I would be very comfortable with him in charge at the saddling paddock," Becky agreed.

Later, Frank spoke to Fred on the phone and gave him their heartfelt condolences. Fred sounded tense and stressed. He didn't mention the race and neither did Frank. They held his wife's memorial service in the winner's circle at Ruidoso Downs, a most fitting place. She was a horse woman through and through. She had done more for New Mexico racing than just about anyone Becky had known. She was kind and helpful to new owners. Sometimes, Becky sat in Fred's box at the track and they visited about the workings of racing. She was the breeder and her husband was the trainer.

Frank, Becky, and friends went to Albuquerque on Friday night—the day before the race so they wouldn't be rushed or late. She had packed twice as much as needed because she couldn't decide how she wanted to look. She had three different fancy hats.

Many of their best friends were sharing the experience. The children and grandchildren were all coming on Saturday. Now Becky was in the position of Grandpa Agard passing on a dream to the next two generations. Win or lose didn't matter. It was the excitement of the total experience for the whole family. It felt like a kind of emotional roller coaster; worry, fear, excitement, hope, and anticipation.

As they stopped by the barn before the races started, Ceasar was in the stall with Thunder. "You better stay close to the Winner's Circle. I have a good feeling about this race." He smiled a big grin.

Everyone went to the Jockey Club. The family had two boxes to start with. Then came more friends from their hometown who had never seen a live horse race before. Becky was amazed they had never seen a horse race before because they were horse people and only lived an hour and a half from the track. Knowing a horse in the race made it different and more exciting. The group had expanded to three boxes and the Jockey Club staff was so kind to let them fill up the space. Becky and Frank's two deaf sons came and brought more friends with them who had also never seen a race live. Becky's enthusiasm and happy chatter about her horse in the "BIG" race had gotten many people to come try a new experience. One hour before the race, the "Thunder Agard" group took up four boxes and the aisles in between. The food and drink servers were so gracious and helpful. They made everyone feel welcome. The group tried to keep themselves contained so as not to bother others, but it was hard.

The big poster of the race program page was at the entrance to the Jockey Club. Frank and Becky took their picture beside it. The boys took their picture beside the poster. It was just a big piece of cardboard with their names on it in bold black letters, but it was exciting to even qualify for such a prestigious race. Other people in the area began to catch the excitement and ask about their horse. Now he was everyone's horse. The kids and grandkids and friends all called Thunder "their" horse. They shared and spoke to everyone. They were the happy, hokey, hillbilly, we've-never-done-this-before type of owners. Some others were the snobby I-know-I'm-important type of owners. The Andersons relished every part of this experience to the fullest and the race hadn't even started yet.

Before post time, Becky's stomach began to ball up and she couldn't focus on all the other people around her. "That's OK," she told herself. They all have their own friends and are doing their own thing, discussing odds and betting and exactas and trifectas. She'd been to the bathroom four times. She didn't want to have to go when she was in the saddling paddock. She worried that she should have worn a different hat. Really! What was wrong with her, she wondered. Just nerves. What if Thunder was dead last with the whole family and so many friends watching? What if this race was too long and he breaks down? What if.....? What if......?

"Stop it!" Becky mentally shouted to herself. She started to make her way to the saddling paddock. The rest of the group spilled out along the rail and bleachers along the track, each one looking for their own spot from which to view the race. She went to stand on the #2 and wait with the other owners. Some shook her hand and wished her good luck.

Thunder came into the saddling paddock with his groom. He was a little more wound up and prancing more than usual. Becky walked over to the stall. Fred, Cesar, and the groom were all there. She again told Fred how sorry they were for his loss. He replied, "She would want me to be here. Racing was important to her." Thunder was a gentleman in the saddling paddock, white saddle blanket with #2 on it, stretchy girth in place, tongue tied and blinkers on. Fred and Becky walk back to the #2 on the circle for owners and trainers. The jockey came out and got brief instructions. This is their favorite jockey for Thunder. He had already ridden him seven times with five wins.

"Jockeys Up" was called. Cesar was riding the pony horse to take him to the post parade and gate with a smile lighting up his face. Faintly, Becky heard the bugle call to post. She walked to the starting gate, which was at the top of the stretch where the bleachers began. She looked down the rail and saw two little towhead kids running by the rail. Her daughter and grandchildren had made it back from Kansas just in time for the post parade as it went by the grandstand.

Becky could see Thunder Agard load into the gate and stand waiting for the others to load. She prayed all went well. The starting gate was where accidents could occur. The start could make or break a race. She could hear the announcer very clearly.

Announcer's call August 23, 2014; The Downs of Albuquerque Race 8 "The Lineage Classic."

"Two back. LE GRANDE'S SPIRIT and the Joel Marr trained favorite, the elegant ON DOWN THE ROAD is in. Set for a start. Off and running for the Lineage classic. A tough beginning for LE GRANDE'S SPIRIT, got pinched slightly at the gate. GOTTA MOVE goes to the front chased by E BAR WAY under a hold with THUNDER AGARD in third. Now slicing through traffic is LE GRANDE'S SPIRIT. PROUD STEP and SPINNING TOUCH. On a hold ON DOWN THE ROAD is back a ways. A tight knit group around the first turn at the casino lounge separated by four lengths. Not much pace up front. E BAR WAY has to take the lead now under a hold from Ruby. Leading is E BAR WAY into the backstretch by a half. GOTTA MOVE is second on a hold. Third is LE GRANDE'S SPIRIT and between fourth is THUNDER AGARD. PROUD STEP is fifth on the rail with no place to go. Now passed by ON DOWN THE ROAD in the clear. Trailing is SPINNING TOUCH. The real racing begins to start as the second half unfolds."

All were jumping up and down and screaming. It didn't look like Thunder was catching up to the leaders, but everyone was encouraging him every step of the way.

"E BAR WAY still leads hounded by LE GRANDE'S SPIRIT second. GOTTA MOVE's all bottled up in third, THUNDER AGARD forth. Wide on the second turn ON DOWN THE ROAD in the five path is coming on. It's a dream run for GOTTA MOVE. Behind trailers SPINNING TOUCH and PROUD STEP."

Becky is screaming at their jockey. "Now! Do it now. Tell Thunder. Let him go." They have already rounded the turn and are on the home stretch. Thunder liked to come from behind, but so did others in this race. The jockey scooted him to the outside and followed the other horse, making his move. At last, the jockey gives Thunder the signal to give it all he's got.

Three taps on the left. Three taps on the right. He'd already used up one third of the stretch. It looked a little too late to catch up from Becky's view. Finally, Thunder bursts his speed and shoots down the track. They are all yelling encouragement. "Come on Thunder. You can do it! Push a little harder! Go! Go.!

Announcer: "E BAR WAY has been cruising throughout. He should have a lot left. The favorite ON DOWN THE ROAD being asked may have his measure. GOTTA MOVE trying. ON DOWN THE ROAD coming on strong strides in a furious rush. THUNDER AGARD is coming on the outside. ON DOWN THE ROAD, E BAR WAY, THUNDER AGARD. THUNDER AGARD, ON DOWN THE ROAD and E BAR WAY. Tremendous finish, three across the road. THUNDER AGARD may have been the fastest in the end. It's a photo for first and second. Please hold all tickets."

Whoosh, they were all so close across the finish line. It looked to Becky like Thunder had pushed about six inches ahead at the finish. All the kids and grandkids were shouting, "We won! We won!" She hadn't been standing on the finish line, so she wasn't sure, but the Photo sign told them it was very close. The family was still cheering and gathering toward the winner's circle. The boys were confident. Becky was shaky and unsure. One of the women in charge of the Lineage presentations stood near the winner's circle with the trophies and exclaimed, "Your grandkids are so excited about this. If they lose in the photo; I'll just have to slit my throat." A little dramatic, but that's how racehorse people talked. The emotion had spread to everyone. Waiting on the official results seemed to take so long, even longer than the race.

Announcer: "#2 THUNDER AGARD in the shadow of the wire wins it in the final jump. 2-7-5-4 official. It's a thrilling winning mile and sixteenth in 1:45.1. The long shot THUNDER AGARD comes through under a heavy ride by Enrique Gomez. 7 to 1 paying 17.50 to win."

Bedlam broke out as everyone rushed to the winner's circle with all of the family and friends, the jockey's wife, child and brother, Cesar's wife and daughter, the Deaf group, and the friends who had never seen a race. Fred and Cesar stood at Thunder's rear end. The groom was holding his head and rubbing his face. The rest were all around the circle to his head about three deep. Everyone had huge smiles. Becky heard someone comment that this was the biggest, happiest winner's circle they had seen in a very long time. One man near the Winner's Circle said that the noise Thunder's crowd was making just held ON DOWN THE ROAD back those few inches.

Becky received her big shiny silver trophy, grinning ear to ear. Fred got a trophy. The jockey got a trophy. *Snap*, the picture was taken. The photographer let the horse go back to the test barn and then took pictures of just the three people with their trophies. Then she took a picture of all the family and friends in a group in the winner's circle. There was a reporter asking Becky questions about Thunder Agard. She hoped she had responded appropriately because she couldn't remember at all what she said.

The big poster from the luncheon was handed to one of the boys. They made their way back to the Jockey Club boxes to share all about the race again. The bettors in the group went to collect their money. The people who had never seen a race before were blown away by the whole experience. It's one they would remember and share for a long time. Several other people in the Jockey Club said, "Thanks. We saw your enthusiasm, so we bet on your horse and we'll have some winnings to take home."

It slowly began to calm down. They watched the final race and everyone went their own way for the moment. Plans were made to meet for family goodbyes at Sunday breakfast. Frank was playing the cool, calm person to Becky's nerves. They made their way down to the barn. Thunder was washed, cooled out, and back in his stall. The test barn vet said he came back in great shape. The longer distance hadn't bothered him at all. Thunder was such a ham. He was hanging his head over the stall gate for more pictures with the trophy and poster. He really wanted to be rubbed behind the ears and to have his food. It was too soon after his race for him to eat. He'd have to wait a couple hours.

"I told you to stay close to the winner's circle," Cesar beamed with a smile that crinkled his whole face while his eyes sparkled. He got a picture of his daughter holding the trophy and Thunder nuzzling her head. This was the biggest race he had trained a horse for from the beginning and won. Fred wasn't back at the barn because he had interviews and well-wishers all over the track. He had finally stopped worrying about Thunder not being able to hold up due to the old injury.

That night, in the quiet of their hotel room, Frank and Becky just held each other. She leaned her head on his chest and listened to his heart beating. "Did you ever think we'd have a Stakes winner?" Frank asked her. He had already watched the replay four times. Becky only watched it once to see how far back Thunder was when he turned loose his burst of speed. He had gained four lengths in the last third of the home stretch. He had tried so hard. She swelled with pride for his effort.

"Yes, I dreamed of a winning race horse, but it started when I was seven and took over fifty years to happen. Grandpa Agard is smiling down from Heaven right now."

It was quiet as they just melted together, spent from all the afternoon excitement. As Frank was starting to drift off to sleep, with his arm around his wife, Becky asked, "Honey, can I breed that mare again?"

Made in the USA
Columbia, SC
05 March 2020

88677624R00071